LIVING
KADDISH

LIVING KADDISH

incredible and inspiring stories

Compiled and edited by
Rabbi Gedalia Zweig

A TARGUM PRESS Book

First published 2007
Copyright © 2007 by Gedalia Zweig
ISBN 978-1-56871-447-9

Published by:
TARGUM PRESS, INC.
22700 W. Eleven Mile Rd.
Southfield, MI 48034
E-mail: targum@targum.com
Fax: 888-298-9992
www.targum.com

Distributed by:
FELDHEIM PUBLISHERS
208 Airport Executive Park
Nanuet, NY 10954

Printing plates by Frank, Jerusalem
Printed in Israel by Chish

28 Nissan 5763
April 30, 2003
Jerusalem, Israel

Rabbi Zweig's book on saying Kaddish has a wonderful flavor that makes it wholesome and incisive for those who have respect for this traditional act of love and honor for the departed. His stories make for interesting and inspirational reading.

Rabbi Noah Weinberg
Rosh Yeshivah, Aish HaTorah, Jerusalem

AISH HATORAH
One Western Wall Plaza
P.O.B. 14149, Old City, Jerusalem, Israel
Tel: (972-2) 628-5666 Fax: (972-2) 627-3172
Email: Jerusalem@aish.com
http://www.aish.com

Even those Jews who have jettisoned their connection to Judaism usually feel compelled to recite Kaddish upon the loss of a relative. Alas, very, very few have any idea what this prayer is all about.

Rabbi Gedalia Zweig, in his masterful and touching collection, unravels the mystery of this prayer and our people's tenacity to its observance. The anecdotes are sure to teach and to touch all those who seek added meaning and understanding at this reflective point in their lives. Surely this book is a fulfillment of the prayer's very credo: "exalting and extolling His great Name."

Rabbi Hanoch Teller
Jerusalem, Israel

May this book assist those in remembering
their beloved ones who have passed on.

In loving memory of our dear brothers and uncles

Neil (Naftali) &
Earl (Yitzchak Zeev)

נפתלי חנן הכהן ז״ל

יצחק זאב הכהן ז״ל

Your beloved brothers Farley & Shlomo Mernick
and your ten loving nieces and nephews

In memory of our dear father

Moishe (Morris) Diamond, *a"h*

l'zichron netzach

For the following *kedoshim*

The Sussman family from Seredna

Ezriel ben Meir

Ester Rachel bat Meir

Dvora Shteinmitz

Yitzchak Izik ben Ezriel

Frumit bat Ezriel

Meir ben Ezriel

Dov (Berel) ben Ezriel

Moshe ben Ezriel

The Diamanstein Family (Uzhorod, Ungvar)

David Shlomo ben Yitzchak Izik

Hena Bat Yehuda

Dov (Berel) ben David Shlomo

Leah bat David Shlomo

Zvi ben David Shlomo

Tshyby bat David Shlomo

Rivka bat David Shlomo

Levi ben David Shlomo

Raizel (Yudit) bat David Shlomo

In loving memory of our dear mother

Penny Benjamin

You were our biggest fan
and we miss you every day

LOVE ALWAYS,
Marc, Stephanie, Jack Penn
and Georgia Benjamin

Dedicated by

Ed Kalkstein and Michael Lax

With thanks to the Forest Hill Jewish Center
Toronto, Canada

Thanks to

Dr. Benji Cooperband
David Koschitzky
Howard Laxton
David Prussky

for their generous support with this book.

Contents

Foreword *17*

Acknowledgments *19*

Introduction *21*

Incredible and Inspiring Stories

Closed for Kaddish 29
  Rabbi Gedalia Zweig

Kaddish Behind Door Number 3 33
  Martin H. Sokol

Colorado Kaddish High 39
  Mark H. Goldenberg

Kaddish by the Candle 41
  Ami Spector

No Kaddish for a Father-in-law 45
  Anyonymous

My JetBlue Minyan 47
  Rabbi Tzvi Konikov

Kaddish in Nunavut 57
  Mark Benjamin

Downhill Kaddish 61
  Frank Cashman

The Tzaddik of Gaza 65
  Anita Tucker

A Momentary Crisis of Faith 69
  Rabbi Yechiel Goldreich

Neither Rain, nor Sleet, nor Blizzards... 71
  Rabbi Asher Herson

Ten Men and a Touchdown. 75
  Max Dekelbaum

Sixteen Months Kaddish 77
  Rabbi Nachum Kook

Kaddish for Ilan 79
  Rabbi Tzvi Konikov

Executive Chesed. 83
  Yisroel Idels

Mission Accomplished!. 87
  Rabbi Gedalia Zweig

In-Flight Kaddish. 91
  Yosi Heber

Lost in the Synagogue 93
  Steve Eigen

I Don't Know about Idaho 97
  Rabbi Dovid Heber

Kaddish for Baby Yehuda 99
  Benni Shoham

The Tenth Man 103
    Sara Karmely

A Second Chance at Kaddish 107
    Menachem Rosenblum

Kaddish at JFK 113
    Rabbi Ari Styner

Remembrance at the Kotel 115
    Michoel Yonasan Sender

Kaddish in the Camps. 117
    Moshe Kraus

Morning at the Minsk. 119
    Rabbi Gedalia Zweig

Kaddish with Oprah. 123
    Simcha Jacobovici

Will Somebody Say Kaddish with Me? 127
    Avron Shore

Concepts of Kaddish

A Practical Guide to Kaddish 133
    Rabbi Gedalia Zweig

Kaddish FAQ's 139
    Rabbi Chanan Yitzchaki

The Mourner's Kaddish 143

Glossary 147

Foreword

Torah provides all the validation necessary for Jewish customs. Nonetheless, it has often been noted how certain Jewish traditions are valid within the construct of psychological theory — even when that theory goes against the grain of human instinct. The two classic examples are the Jewish practices of *bikur cholim*, visiting the sick, and *aveilut*, mourning.

In the secular world, when one visits a hospital patient, all conversation focuses on the patient's ailment: "How do you feel?" "What medication are you taking?" "When is the surgery?" Although these questions are instinctual, they unnecessarily keep the patient focused on pain, fear, and mortality. But when a Jew enacts the mitzvah of *bikur cholim*, the visitor attempts to speak about all manner of subjects to keep the patient's mind off his ailment, lifting the patient's spirit and (according to the Gemara in *Berachot*) removing one-sixtieth of the patient's illness.

The converse is true in a *shivah* house, a house of mourning. Instinct drives us to speak to the mourners about anything but the deceased in order to divert their attention from their loss. But a *shivah* call paid properly is one where the visitor listens to the mourners recount stories about the departed loved one, highlighting his virtues, and generally helps them come to grips with their loss.

But as cathartic as seven days spent focusing exclusively on the deceased is, the mourners do not "get up" from *shivah* fully emotionally healed. More time is necessary to remember the departed and to honor his or her memory.

This is where the Mourner's Kaddish comes in. By reciting the daily Kaddish seven times a day for eleven months, the mourner takes a few moments out from each day to remember and honor the deceased loved one.

The stories in this book are inspiring not because they are mystical; these stories are inspiring — emotionally and religiously — because they are stories of powerful, enduring love, the love that children feel for their parents and that parents feel for their children, the love of siblings and the love of spouses. And, perhaps most importantly, these stories represent the love that Jews feel for G-d, a love so great that we embrace it in our most vulnerable hours — by reciting His praise as we mourn our loss of a mortal life and, in so doing, acknowledging an immortal soul.

Rabbi Mayer Waxman
Director, Synagogue Services
Orthodox Union

Acknowledgments

I want to thank all the *rabbanim* who have seen me through this project. Thank you, Rav Moshe Stern, for your support and guidance. To Rav Mayer Waxman, a thousand thanks for your help and inspiration. To my *rosh yeshivah*, Rav Noah Weinberg of Jerusalem, thank you for instilling in me a love of Judaism, which gave me the impetus to publish this book. A special thanks to Rabbi Hanoch Teller for all your insights.

I also want to thank all those who inspired me not to miss a Kaddish, like Brian, who missed only one Kaddish — when he was in Sarnia, Ontario, where very few Jews live. Or Dov, who made every Kaddish but one — while on vacation in the United States, but only because on the way to Brookline, Massachusetts, he made a right turn when he should have made a left, thereby missing a *minchah* service. Or the fellow who worked at Toronto's Lester B. Pearson International Airport — far away from any minyanim — and did not miss a single service.

The following people have helped me so much with the editing and proofreading: Sarah Bedein, Rachel Lefkowitz, Shelly Herman, and Joseph Heller. Gil Kezwer, thank you for your thoughts. Sander Shalinsky, thanks for all your help. And an extra thanks to my great copy editor Daniel Wolgelerenter. Many thanks to Miriam Zakon, Suri Brand, and Beena Sklare of Targum Press for their great expertise.

I'd also like to thank my dear wife, Grace, for her gracious support, and my son Naftali for letting me use your (our) computer.

Finally, thanks to the Almighty for letting me reach this goal.

And you, the reader, I ask that once you finish this book, please lend it to someone who thinks they don't need it. If one person learns something from it, my efforts in putting it together will have been worth it.

Introduction

March 1, 2002, Adar 18. I'll always remember that horrible day. Not only did my mother, *aleha hashalom*, pass away — it was also the beginning of the worst month of terrorism during the recent intifada in the Middle East. There was news of suicide bombings and terror victims daily. I was actually happy that my mother was not around to hear all of this disturbing news, because I knew it would have been terribly distressing for her.

That Shabbat, March 2, 2002, eleven people were murdered at a bar mitzvah near Meah Shearim. The day of the funeral, that Sunday, March 3, ten soldiers were killed at a roadblock near Ofra in Samaria. On March 5, three people were murdered in another terror attack. On March 7, five youths were killed at a yeshivah in Gush Katif. On March 9, eleven people were killed at the Moment Café in Jerusalem. March 12, six people were killed near Kibbutz Metzuba; March 14, three soldiers were killed near the Gaza Strip in a tank by a land mine; March 20, seven people were blown up on an Egged bus from Tel Aviv to Nazareth; March 21, three people, including a pregnant woman, were executed by a suicide bomber in Jerusalem; and on March 27, twenty-nine people (the most in a single attack) were annihilated at a Passover seder at a hotel in Netanya.

As I began the process of saying Kaddish for my mom, it gained an even deeper significance and I felt an even deeper sadness because I felt I was saying it not only for her, but also for all of the Israeli victims of terror.

For the rest of that year, my day revolved around saying Kaddish. I would get up early and leave work early to catch a minyan. I would make sure that I was at shul promptly on Friday night and on Shabbat morning. As a consequence of saying the Kaddish prayer three times a day over such an extended period of time, it became like a poetic refrain in my mind, each word bearing its own significance.

Our trip to Orlando that year was challenging for my family. I was in my eleventh month of Kaddish when we took that much-needed vacation, which we had booked before my mother died. After September 11, travel had become more difficult than it used to be, and in addition, no matter where we were, we had to ensure that I would be able to find a minyan. However, if I had to do that trip all over again, I wouldn't change a thing. Because I was in a city that is home to twenty thousand Jews, I was always able to find a minyan — sometimes in unusual places — and I met some really interesting people.

At the end of my year of saying Kaddish, I felt that something was missing in my life. That period of time held so much significance for me and my brother Arnie. All the trials and tribulations of seeking out minyanim left a very personal imprint on my life. I knew that I needed to fill the void with something very meaningful. I felt a sense of urgency to not only share my Kaddish experiences with others, but to hear and convey the unique stories that others have experienced during their Kaddish journeys.

I decided to send e-mails to 1,000 Orthodox Union–affiliated synagogues, as well as to Chabad houses and Aish HaTorah branches, asking people to share their Kaddish stories with me. I also sent letters to Jewish newspapers in North America and e-mailed Hebron, Shilo, Gush Katif, Efrat, and friends in Jerusalem. I received many wonderful and heartening responses, which inspired me to collect them in a book and share these stories with others.

Many well-meaning Jews try to say Kaddish at least seven times a day (depending on custom) during the eleven-month period of mourning for a parent. But Kaddish can be a bit like dating: many people give up after a few months. As the stories in this book attest, with G-d's help you can say Kaddish for the entire eleven months and carry on right through to the *yahrtzeit*, the first anniversary of your parent's passing.

Enjoy the stories that follow, and may we all be inspired and uplifted by them. If anyone has a story to share, please e-mail me at kaddishstory@hotmail.com. For a list of minyanim around the world, visit www.godaven.com. For practical advice and laws and customs, see "Concepts of Kaddish" at the back of this book.

I dedicate this book to my dear Mom

Chaya Rachel bat Naftali

and to all those killed through terrorism

Incredible and Inspiring Kaddish Stories

Closed for Kaddish

Rabbi Gedalia Zweig

Toronto, Canada

Reb Naftali Reingewirtz, my mother's father, started our family's paint store in March 1929. It began as a small operation in the family living room, but over the years it became one of the busiest paint suppliers in downtown Toronto. It's now located on Baldwin Street, in a neighborhood known as Kensington Market, where much of the Jewish community once lived and many shuls were once located. My father, who was not an observant Jew, joined the business in 1952. When my mother died on March 1, 2002, I felt obligated to carry on the tradition.

Many businessmen face challenges with Kaddish. In wintertime, davening is so early; in summertime it is very late. Because my father lost his parents and three sisters in the Holocaust, I was not about to give up on saying Kaddish. Friday afternoon was the most difficult time for me. When my dad ran the store, I could always leave early for Shabbat. But when I became manager, I had to close the store at 4 p.m. on Fridays. With sunset around 4:45 p.m. on this particular *erev Shabbat*, I figured I had enough time to get home for *minchah*. I was already dressed — I had brought my Shabbat clothes with me downtown. All I had to do was get to shul.

As I left the store to begin what would normally be a forty-minute drive to my home in Thornhill, a suburb just north of Toronto's city boundary, one thing I hadn't counted on was traffic. I zoomed up Bathurst Street, the city's main north-south artery of Jewish life since the community began migrating north in the 1950s, but I had to slow down to a crawl when I passed St. Clair Avenue, the point where the concentration of Jewish homes, businesses, and synagogues begins to significantly increase.

While it was inspiring to see the splendor of Toronto's Jewish community, particularly as it prepared for Shabbat, it was becoming increasingly clear to me that I wasn't going to make it home before sundown. I realized I'd have to stop and find the nearest shul. After passing Finch Avenue, I practically dived into Congregation Bnai Torah, a midsized Orthodox shul in the northern end of the city. Rabbi Raphael Marcus, the son-in-law of the great scholar Rabbi Aharon Soloveitchik, has been the *rav* there for more than twenty years.

As I raced into shul, panting, I was greeted by Rabbi Marcus's warm smile.

He was the officiating rabbi at my wedding, so the first thing he asked was, "Is everything all right at home?"

"All is well. Just get me to the minyan on time," I replied.

"We're already starting *Kabbalat Shabbat*. I'm sorry, but you've missed *minchah*!"

I practically jumped up in the air. "I can't! I must say Kaddish for my mother, and I haven't missed one yet!"

He motioned to Izzy Kaplan, the owner of Israel's Judaica and one of the community leaders.

"Make a minyan in the hallway," Rabbi Marcus said to Izzy.

Afterward, I caught a glimpse of Michael Stavsky, my wife's coworker.

"What brings you to our parts?" he asked.

"Well, I ran out of time, so I'm here," I confessed sheepishly.

After davening, I left my wallet and keys in Rabbi Marcus's podium and walked forty-five minutes to my home. It just so happened that I had invited a guest for that night's meal, Michael Rosen, whom I had run into at a gas station the week before. We had been together in Israel twenty years earlier. When I finally arrived, he and my wife asked why I was so late. I explained, and they both understood.

There's an interesting postscript to this story. The following Monday, representatives from Benjamin Moore, our number one paint supplier, came to our store to check out if we merited becoming a franchise.

I was a little unsure about what would happen. But guess what? It was the busiest Monday I had ever seen at the store in the winter. Customers came in one after the other from 9 a.m. till noon. Many of them asked, "Why did you close early on Friday?"

When the Benjamin Moore reps were getting ready to leave, they commented, "Wow, this store sure is busy!"

I just smiled.

I am convinced the Almighty made the day such a success because of the way I honored Kaddish (and closed early) the previous Friday.

The following week I avoided being caught in the same mad dash. I found a Friday minyan at 1 p.m. at Mount Sinai Hospital, a mere five minutes east by foot from my shop. Seek and ye shall find!

Kaddish Behind Door Number 3

Martin H. Sokol

Brussels, Belgium

In November 1993, the American Thanksgiving holiday weekend and my mother's *yahrtzeit* coincided. Our son, Joe, had recently graduated with honors from college and elected to go into the family leather merchant business. I suggested he learn the technical components of leather tanning by attending a well-respected leather school in Northampton, England, outside London. When my wife suggested we visit Joe during Thanksgiving, it made sense. I would lose little business time, it would be fun, and, of course, we missed our son. The only problem, it occurred to me, was that I had to say Kaddish for my mother while in Europe.

Our visit to Joe would include business. I worked in international leather trading, and one of our important suppliers was Europe's oldest tannery, located in Belgium. The tannery manufactures high-grade leathers to leather goods companies such as the Louis Vuitton group.

Davening in London was no problem, and we chose a hotel within walking distance to London's Marble Arch Synagogue, and coincidentally also to Buckingham Palace. In London, I would daven *shacharit* and *ma'ariv*. The only question was *minchah*. Would I be able to find a minyan in Brussels? I davened *ma'ariv* and *shacharit* at the Marble Arch Synagogue and immediately upon arrival in Brussels asked the concierge where I could find a synagogue. He gave me an address. I immediately hired a limousine, and the three of us were driven to the shul.

When we arrived, all the doors were locked. I searched around the building and finally found a bell on a door. After a few rings, someone answered — an elderly man whom I assumed was a caretaker. He informed me that his synagogue rarely had a minyan, and unless someone reserved one in advance, there was none. He suggested another street where I would be more likely to find one.

It was getting late. I had not expected the delay. We gave the new address to the chauffeur and drove on. When we arrived at the street where my minyan was supposed to be, there was no synagogue to be found. We went up and down the street a few times, but no building indicated it was a synagogue. At the point of giving up, I noticed four men leaving a store and entering a car. I walked over to the car and asked in English if they knew of a synagogue in the area. They replied that there were none in this particular area and asked, "Why would you want a synagogue?" Since they were all wearing either hats or caps, I took a chance and asked them if they knew what Kaddish was. They smiled and said, "Of course. We are all Jews." After briefly explaining that I needed to say Kaddish for my mother, one of the men said, "Follow my car."

My chauffeur thought I was taking a risk following strangers, but I told my wife and son, "How risky could it be following strangers to a minyan?"

Soon we arrived at a commercial district where streets were made of cobblestone and all the buildings were old warehouses. Dusk was approaching. It had rained only an hour before, and the area was totally devoid of people. One of the men got out of the car, pointed to a gray steel door, and said, "Go in there," and then quickly sped off.

I told my wife, Judy, and my son to stay in the car and walked up to the steel door. There were no signs on the building, not even an address. Just an old brick building with a gray steel door and a buzzer, which I rang. The buzzer responded. I opened the gray door, which was hinged to a strong spring, and it shut quickly behind me.

I was now in a vestibule made of thick bulletproof glass, the same glass bank tellers often sit behind. Immediately after entering, I heard a stern, no-nonsense voice with an Israeli accent ask over a loudspeaker, "Who are you?"

I replied, in typical Jewish fashion, with a question of my own. "Where am I?"

The speaker replied, "What do you want?"

"Someone said I could find a minyan here. I want to say

Kaddish for my mother. It's her *yahrtzeit*."

Two men quickly came into view. Both held Uzi submachine guns. One came out into the vestibule area.

He proceeded to ask me some questions. He asked to see my passport. And then he asked me a series of questions that pertain to Judaism that only a Jew would know. I don't recall the questions, but they went something like, How old was I when I was bar mitzvah? When is Shabbat? How many questions do we ask on Passover? Things like that.

I passed the test, and the guards said I could enter the area behind the bulletproof glass enclosure. I asked if I could bring my wife and son, who were waiting for me in the car.

When I returned to the car, I told my wife and son that someone inside said I would find a minyan inside, but I didn't see any people except for two security guards holding Uzi submachine guns. "Don't worry, I believe they are Israelis," I said.

When the three of us entered the building, the security guards buzzed us through the two doors, and then buzzed us through a third door where they said I would find a minyan.

I opened the third security door and what I heard and saw reminded me of a scene out of the Wizard of Oz, the one where Dorothy enters the Technicolor fantasyland of Oz and the movie changes from the "real" world of black and white to color.

Behind the third security door was a totally different kingdom. Music — Jewish music — was being played. Behind the third door, children were laughing and singing. Mothers and fathers were doing the same. Where was I?

I walked over to one adult and asked in French (I don't speak French, but this much I knew), "Do you speak English?"

The man replied, "Yes."

"Where am I? What is going on?"

The man looked at me very suspiciously and quickly went over to another group of men. They approached me and asked what I was doing here. I replied that someone said I could find a minyan there because I wanted to say Kaddish for my mother.

The story of my search for a Kaddish minyan ends here. The factory building was a yeshivah. That Sunday was the celebration of its opening. The site was probably chosen for security purposes. A few months earlier the leader of the Brussels Jewish community was shot and killed by PLO terrorists. The Jews of Brussels had to be cautious.

When I found out where I was and thought of the strict security these children and grandchildren of Holocaust survivors had to endure, I was unable to speak. Tears filled my eyes. My throat was choked with emotion. I could not stop thinking that fewer than fifty years after the Holocaust, Jews were once again in danger in Europe.

When I returned to New York, I recounted this Kaddish saga to my friends, but the story, for at least a few months, was always interrupted with a pause. Even today, emotion gets the better of me when I think of that dismal factory building, the three security doors, the Israeli guards with Uzis contrasting with children dancing and singing Hebrew songs.

For me, the experience symbolized our long, troubled history. Kaddish is said to remember people we loved who are no longer alive. The guards remind me of how, throughout history, when we chose to fight back, we lived. The children help me to remember that we have survived and that there will always be another generation who will remember, who will fight to retain our precious heritage, who will say Kaddish.

Colorado Kaddish High

Mark H. Goldenberg

Aspen, Colorado

I've had the pleasure of leading the Seders and davening for Pesach in resorts around the world for more than twenty years. For Pesach 1993, we were in beautiful Aspen, Colorado, at the Ritz-Carlton Hotel. With us were approximately two hundred people who had come to get in their last skiing of the season. Skiing in Aspen is always glorious, but at Pesach time it's spectacular. My most vivid memory was taking my lunch break and opening the lunch box the hotel gave us to take along. As usual, there was a little matzah, cheese, a hard-boiled egg, certainly nothing gourmet. But sitting under the beautiful blue skies with a view of the snow-capped mountains, I thought never had matzah tasted so good. It's a *chol hamo'ed* experience I'll never forget.

As one of the religious leaders of the group, along with Rabbi Alan Kalinsky, the West Coast director of the Orthodox Union, I got to know everyone on the program. On Shabbat *chol hamo'ed,* between *minchah* and *ma'ariv,* in walked a man with a *kapote,* hat, and beard. I asked Rabbi Kalinsky if he knew who the man was. It turned out his name was Rabbi Yehoshua Witt.

As soon as I heard the name, I realized that this man had been my high school classmate in Skokie, Illinois, many years before. Because of the change in his appearance, it wasn't until I heard his name that I knew who he was.

Rabbi Witt had grown up in Aspen, became a *ba'al teshuvah,* and now lived in Jerusalem with his wife and children. His father had passed away that week, and he had flown in for the funeral. There was no minyan at the funeral, so he couldn't recite Kaddish for his father at the grave site. Since it was Pesach, and he had no food arrangements in Aspen, he came to town with only a box of matzah and jars of gefilte fish. He had planned to leave for New York immediately after Shabbat. Much to his amazement, he heard there was a group celebrating Pesach in the hotel, so he came to check it out. He was able to say Kaddish with a minyan, have fresh kosher-for-Pesach food, and spend Pesach in the proper manner in Aspen, of all places. A week earlier or later, and he would not have had access to a minyan, nor the kosher food.

Hashem works in amazing ways.

Kaddish by the Candle

Ami Spector

Holon, Israel

My father, Avraham Spector was nineteen years old when he arrived in Israel and settled in Beersheva. The year was 1947, and his whole family had been killed in Poland in the Holocaust. When he arrived in the Holy Land, he said to his wife, "There is no G-d!"

When I was born, my mother insisted on naming me after his father, Israel. But my father said, "No. I am not convinced he is dead!" They compromised and named me Ami, from the phrase "*Am Yisrael chai* — The people of Israel live!"

It was the day before Purim 1965. My mother was getting ready for a costume party at the school. She waited for my father to return home from work, and he was anxious to get home to be with his new six-month-old son. But on the way a car veered into his lane, right in front of him. To avoid a head-on collision, he swerved and his car flipped over into a ditch. The steering wheel pierced his lungs.

Amazingly, he walked away as the ambulance came. "Take care of the other injured," he said. "I'll be all right."

But when he came home, he felt worse and wanted to go to the hospital. Sadly, he never made it. My father died at the age of thirty-seven, leaving behind a child who never knew him.

When I went to school at age 4, I realized that I had no father. Just like there was a fat kid and a smart kid and a stupid kid, I was "the kid with no father."

By this time, we were living in Holon. When I was twelve, it was time for me to study for my bar mitzvah. A rabbi in town taught me my haftorah. For the first time, I saw a Hebrew book like no other, a book containing the prayers I would say for the bar mitzvah. I wanted to find more books like that, but I could not find any in Holon. One day I traveled into the city and saw a large table of used books at a book fair. I thought for sure I would find my book there. And I did! I was very excited. I could now pray every day.

The week before my bar mitzvah, my grandmother took me to my father's grave for the first time. I noticed a few poor people around asking for charity. My grandmother took some change out of her purse and motioned for them to come along. When they arrived at the stone, I realized what she was trying to do. She was trying to get a minyan together so I could say Kaddish for the first time. I turned to page 97 of my siddur, where I found the Mourner's Kaddish, and said it in honor of my father.

From the age of thirteen till thirty, I would follow this custom. The night before Purim I would light a candle and hold a picture of my dad. Then I would recite the Kaddish prayer by candlelight. By myself. No minyan.

I did not have a religious upbringing. I had gone to shul only two times in my life: at my bar mitzvah and at my wedding. After I married, my wife and I moved to Toronto. When my first child returned home from Jewish day care and started kissing the mezuzah and saying Shema, I almost went through the roof. My wife, Vered, calmed me down.

"We are now in Toronto. This is what Jews do here. If you don't want your son to see a hypocrite in the house, you had better shape up."

That year, 1992, I went to shul for the first time on Rosh HaShanah. That year, on the *yahrtzeit* of my father, I said Kaddish with a minyan for the first time.

I've done it every year since.

No Kaddish for a Father-in-law

Anonymous

Bnei Brak, Israel

I want to remain anonymous, but I feel that by sharing this story, I can be an inspiration to other sons-in-law.

Six years ago my father-in-law passed away. He had no sons — his only two children are my wife and her sister. At the time, my parents were still alive, so I could not say Kaddish for my father-in-law. I loved him very much and felt that I had somehow "wronged" him by moving to Israel a month and a half after my wife and I had married. He was a long-distance father, father-in-law, and grandfather for some twenty-four years. I felt I owed him.

I davened at the *amud* (led the services) for the entire year, missing only two *tefillot* during the *shivah* week and maybe a *tefillah* or two on the High Holidays. Mind you, I'm talking about every davening — including Shabbat, *yom tov*, Rosh HaShanah, and Yom Kippur. Lucky for me, at the time I was the chazzan for *mussaf* in my shul for the High Holidays. But you can't believe the problems I faced, not being truly obligated. Anyone with a *yahrtzeit* could knock me out of the chazzan's box, which is what happened many times. Luckily for me, I live in Bnei Brak and was able to fall back on the Itzkowitz Shul for the *amud*. There, no questions are asked. You wait on line and then you get the *amud*.

I was once davening before the *amud* when I eyed someone coming down the road holding a bag and his tallis. I knew that the bag signaled the end of the *amud* for me: in it were cake and whiskey. I hightailed it down to the next shul and got the *amud* there.

My motto during the entire year was "Have fallback minyan, will daven." My father-in-law, of blessed memory, was well worth the effort.

I hope my story inspires others who can't say Kaddish for whatever reason. Davening before the *amud* is a great *zechut* and you don't need to be an *avel* to do it.

My JetBlue Minyan

Rabbi Tzvi Konikov

Satellite Beach, Florida

I am on my way to Israel on El Al for a bar mitzvah of one of our Chabad members. It's 11:30 p.m., and, along with 450 other passengers, I am trying to get as comfortable as possible for the long flight to the Holy Land. My mind is reeling. I still can't believe what happened to me just a few hours ago!

I was attending services daily, saying Kaddish in memory of my mother. JetBlue Flight 46 from Orlando to JFK en route to Israel presented a challenge.

Rabbi Chaim Tzvi Konikov serves as spiritual leader and director of Chabad of the Space & Treasure Coasts in Florida.

The connecting flight schedules were very tight, so I arranged with my brother, Rabbi Aaron Levi Konikov, that he would take me from JFK to his Roslyn, New York, Chabad Center for afternoon services.

I had covered all possibilities — or so I thought. In Yiddish there's an expression, *"Mensch tracht und G-t lacht —* Man proposes and G-d disposes."* This was a perfect example. We were supposed to depart Orlando at 4:15 p.m., but the captain announced a ninety-minute delay due to bad weather.

I had not missed saying one Kaddish since my mother passed away ten months ago. What to do?

Worried, I thought, *I'll exit the plane. I'll miss the flight. I can always rebook, but I can't miss Kaddish.*

I went up to a stewardess. "Excuse me, I have an important meeting in New York, and if I can't make it in person, I must leave the plane right now."

"I'm sorry," she replied politely. "We cannot return to the gate. We are on the runway waiting to take off. There are planes ahead of us and planes behind us. We cannot move. It's impossible."

Oh, well. I tried.

Thirty minutes passed and we were going nowhere.

Every few seconds, I looked at my watch and calculated our earliest possible arrival time. Another fifteen minutes passed. I realized I must do something, but what?

Suddenly, a crazy thought dawned on me. *Maybe there are enough Jews on this flight to make a minyan!* I didn't notice any religious Jews, but it was my only hope.

Before I make a scene, I'll check my chances of success, I told myself.

Trying to be inconspicuous, I got up from my seat "to stretch" and walked up and down the aisles looking for Jewish faces. Alas, only the guy in the last seat had a Jewish face. And I wasn't even sure about him. Was I dreaming or was I so desperate that I imagined he looked Jewish?

I gathered my courage and asked him straight out, "Are you Jewish?" I almost hit the roof when he answered, "Yes!"

Quickly, I explained that I had to say Kaddish for my mother and needed a minyan.

He understood. "Count me in when you get ten," he replied. Then he resumed his reclining position in front of the TV, nodding his head slightly to wish me good luck.

Bolstered by my success, I identified the next "Jewish face." Before I knew it, we were up to four! Each commented, "I'm not religious," or "I don't know how to pray." Still, they were willing to help.

The minutes continued to tick by, but I had run into a brick wall. That was it for Jewish faces. How many people who looked Puerto Rican could possibly be Jewish? Should I call it a day? Give up? Seat by seat I made my plea, but this time a little bit different than before.

"Excuse me, is anyone in your party Jewish?" I asked. And the unbelievable was happening. Once in a while, the answer was "Yes, he is," or "Yes, I am."

By this time, I had seven. *Only three more to go*, I thought to myself. Surprisingly, one of JetBlue's managers was sitting in a regular seat. "Can I help you?" he asked. I thought he was just following the customer service routine. But when I explained my predicament, he immediately sprung into action to help me. Amazingly, he offered to make an announcement asking for volunteers over the PA system.

"Thank you," I answered. "But I'm going to try to do this low profile."

"Excuse me," the man across from the aisle spoke up. "I overheard your conversation. I am Jewish."

Now we had eight! I was beginning to believe it would happen. I continued my search. I began to get excited at the prospect of a miraculous minyan. But a bunch of people saying "Sorry" and "No" brought me back to reality. One passenger who really wanted to help but wasn't Jewish said to me, "My buddy is half-Jewish."

Hopefully, I asked his friend, "Are you Jewish?"

"No, not really," he answered.

Disappointed, I turned to walk away. "But my grandmother was Jewish!" he added.

I turned and asked, "Your mother's mother?"

"Yeah, but that doesn't make me Jewish, does it?"

"You bet it does!" I told him.

"Neat! Just like that, I find out I'm Jewish! Maybe the delay was worth it, just for that!"

At T-minus one Yid and counting, I was roaring down the aisle with confidence now, ready to launch this nearly made minyan. By this time, no one on the plane had any doubts as to what was happening. Every so often the manager would call out to me, "How many are we up to?" When I told him we were at nine, he radioed to the cockpit and asked if any of the crew was Jewish. "Negative" came the reply.

At this point, everyone wanted to help, but the situation seemed hopeless. I had already gone through every seat twice, and the dark reality seemed to be settling in that there were only nine male Jews over the age of thirteen on this plane.

As I was making my way back to my seat, crestfallen,

someone who felt very sorry for me stopped me and said: "I have a Jewish friend in Georgia who I can call on a conference. Will that work?"

I explained and thanked him anyway. (As if I didn't know a few Jews myself that I could phone!)

I called my brother, Rabbi Yosef Konikov of Chabad of South Orlando, telling him the whole story. "You won't believe this: we've got nine people for this minyan. But that's really it," I said anxiously. "You're a chaplain in the sheriff's department. Maybe you can get someone Jewish from security to come out here and get onto the plane with us."

He said he would try, but he didn't sound too hopeful. Time and the odds were both working against us.

If I don't make this minyan after finding nine Jews on this flight, what a letdown it will be, I said to myself.

Mentally, I was preparing myself for exactly that letdown because I had run out of options. I returned to my seat, just waiting to see what would happen next.

A few seconds passed before the passenger right behind me cleared his throat and confessed, "I'm really sorry, but earlier, when I told you I was not Jewish, I wasn't telling the truth. I was just very intimidated. I really am Jewish."

My eyes became as wide as saucers. At first I thought that he was pulling my leg. Either that or he was just trying to be nice because he saw how desperate I was. I was suspicious, and I knew I had to do a little questioning.

"Is your mother Jewish?" I asked conversationally (as if I had all the time in the world!).

"Absolutely," he responded. "Her maiden name is Horowitz. You can't get more Jewish than that!" Then he added, "There's no question. I even know the words of *Barchu*."

Everyone around me became giddy with excitement. I signaled my loyal and devoted JetBlue manager who was sitting about ten rows behind me. "It's a go!" I cried. "We've got ten!"

You would have thought he had just won the lotto, that's how happy he was for me.

The manager invited me to meet with the stewardesses at the back of the plane. He wanted to make sure that the minyan would go smoothly. I went back and told them that there really wasn't much that I needed and that I did not want to inconvenience them whatsoever. I suggested that they finish serving the beverages before we'd start so we wouldn't get in their way. Other than that, I told them that the afternoon prayer would take between seven and nine minutes altogether. I also thanked them for their help and understanding.

The manager offered to let me know once they finished making their rounds through the plane. He would also help me gather my nine volunteers. As soon as I got the word from the manager, I started going down the aisles "picking up" people. (I was hoping I'd remember who they were! I did.)

It didn't take very long before a line of Jews was walking behind me toward the back. About three rows before the end of the plane, I noticed a face I had missed. *He certainly looks Jewish,* I thought. *With all these unknown people, maybe it's best to have eleven men, just in case.*

So I stopped and asked him, "Are you Jewish?"

He said, "Yes, but look, you're holding up the aisle! All these people want to get by!"

I said, "These people are my minyan!"

Astonished, he quickly got into the spirit. "Well, then, I'm coming, too!"

The atmosphere at the back of the plane was electric. The Jewish men were giving each other high fives. You would have thought they had just won the NBA title!

We packed into the tiny galley kitchen in the back of the plane. The stewardesses barely had room to stand with us, so I politely suggested that they stand in front of us "to make sure no one disturbs the service." They happily obliged.

Before the minyan started, I briefed the nonreligious members about what we were going to do. From their blank looks, it appeared that only three of the eleven people had ever participated in a minyan before.

While my main objective was to say Kaddish, I didn't want the experience for these secular Jews to be just lip service. I took the opportunity to say a quick short word on the concept of prayer.

"Prayer is not restricted to a particular place but can be done anywhere, from the privacy of your own room to a JetBlue plane that is stuck on the runway," I told them. Then I got to the nitty-gritty. "Since JetBlue does not, as yet, have ten prayer books for in-flight services, I will lead the service in Hebrew by heart. The only thing I ask is that you say 'Amen' at the right time."

"How will we know when it's the right time if you're saying it in Hebrew?" one passenger asked.

It was a good question. "I'll give you the thumbs-up when it's time," I responded.

I took my *kippah* from under my hat and handed it to one of the men nearest me. The rest of the men made themselves at home in the kitchen and distributed *kippot* (napkins, actually) — compliments of JetBlue.

The scene was awesome. Without further delay, I launched our minyan.

I felt like a million bucks when I gave my first thumbs-up. I was all choked up in gratitude to G-d.

The "Amens" were loud and emphatic. This bunch was definitely not shy or embarrassed of their heritage. I felt like I was back in camp leading the bunk competition. The whole plane was buzzing. Napkin-covered men shouting "Amen" at each thumbs-up of this ancient-looking rabbi — it was definitely not the typical scene in a JetBlue advertisement!

Despite the obvious humor of the situation, the men seemed quite touched and stayed focused and serious throughout the prayers. I finished the davening and thanked everyone profusely for their time. Then we returned to our seats.

Almost immediately, the pilot announced that the delay was over. In minutes we would be departing for JFK. The feeling was incredible. It was almost as if the minyan was part of the schedule. (Of course, the minyan was part of the schedule that G-d keeps for us!)

After the plane was in the air, one of the Jews from the minyan came over to my aisle seat. With tears in his eyes, he said, "I am totally uninvolved in Judaism, and I want to thank you deeply for this awesome reminder of my heritage."

Now it was my turn to be humbled. It's amazing how one mitzvah leads to the next! What an unbelievable way to start my trip to the Holy Land!

Later, my wife and I discussed the incredible story. We agreed that although this year of Kaddish had a number of novel stories and extremely close calls, this one was on a "plane" by itself!

My wife told her sisters in New York what had happened. They, of course, repeated it to their husbands. One of them,

Rabbi Levi Baumgarten, serves as the "Mitzvah Tank rabbi" (with the Chabad Mitzvah Mobile) in Manhattan. He was scheduled to meet one of his steady "customers" a week later in the Mitzvah Tank. This customer was a very successful businessman working for Cushman & Wakefield.

As the man stepped into the Mitzvah Tank, he said to Rabbi Baumgarten, "Do I have a story to tell you! I just heard from my JetBlue associates. They were returning from a big corporate meeting in Orlando last Tuesday and a rabbi was on the plane."

Levi smiled. "Let me finish the story..."

"But how?" he asked, dumbfounded by the rabbi's certainty.

Rabbi Baumgarten replied, "All Jews are connected. The Jewish world is very small, and we are all brothers. The rabbi who needed the minyan on JetBlue last week is my brother-in-law!"

Kaddish in Nunavut

Mark Benjamin

Northwest Territories, Canada

I've been going on canoe trips since I was ten years old. Each year, the trips seem to get longer and harder. Our canoe trip in the summer of 2002 was one I will never forget. (Actually, you never forget a canoe trip, even the "bad" ones, if there is such a thing.)

For starters, we would be canoeing the historic Hood River located in Nunavut in the Arctic, the river made famous by Sir John Franklin's 1845 expedition to find the Northwest Passage. Our starting point would be a small lake with no name, marked only by its elevation of 414 meters (1,240 feet) above sea level. We would be picked up by floatplane in Bathurst Inlet, a tiny place with a population of about twenty located in the Arctic Ocean.

Another thing that made the trip memorable for me was our minyan. We recruit fifteen to twenty friends each year. We usually end up with six or eight people (an even number is needed for running rapids), but this year we had ten, meaning five boats, five tents, and lots of food.

It also meant I could say Kaddish.

You see, my mother passed away the previous fall at the age of fifty-four so I was still in my year of mourning. I had been going to synagogue twice daily, whether I was at home or on vacation. Knowing what our usual turnout was like, I didn't know what I was going to do about saying Kaddish. But it happened all on its own — without making a request for ten paddlers, that's exactly what we got.

The trip would last fifteen days on the river. We would paddle past huge ice fields that had not yet retreated from the previous winter. We saw musk ox, caught fish at will, and shot countless sets of raging rapids, were in awe at the indescribable sight of Wilberforce Falls.

Before I shoot any set of rapids, I get very nervous. But throughout this entire trip I had an overwhelming feeling of assurance that the canoe would not overturn. I truly felt that my mother was watching over me and guiding my canoe. I was still nervous before every set. I still had to scout the set to see what lay ahead and to plan the best route. I still had to respect the fact that I was above the Arctic Circle and that overturning in the frigid waters (38 degrees Fahrenheit) could be disastrous. But I knew I was not going to tip. Even when a friend and I decided to lower our canoe into the canyon below Wilberforce

Falls and paddle our way out, the feeling and knowledge that she was with me, that we would paddle it through without incident, was always there. It was very reassuring.

The memory I have taken away from this expedition, one that will never leave me, is of the last night on the river. We had woken up that day to a strong headwind funneling down to the river from the ocean. This meant that for every forward stroke we made, the wind would push us back two strokes. During the Arctic summer, it never gets any darker than a normal dusk. We decided to relax at the campsite and wait until the winds calmed down before we made our final push to the ocean. We got in our canoes at 8 p.m., but with the amount of light out, you would have thought it was one in the afternoon.

We arrived at our final destination, where our planes would be meeting us the next morning, the place where the tundra ends and the Arctic Ocean begins. This was to be our final campsite. By this time it was after midnight. We set up camp and made our second fire of the trip (since we were above the tree line, there were no trees to burn), and I found a comfortable place to daven. When it was time for Kaddish, it was well after 1 a.m. and the period of dusk had begun. There were no trees or mountains to obstruct the view, and the sun was setting to my left.

The sunset was magical, crimson and gold, and it seemed to stretch for thousands of miles. The entire northwestern sky was on fire, and I found myself surrounded by the sunset as I prayed. This was a place where I could feel that my mother was truly with me, a place where I could feel God's Presence — a place of indescribable beauty, harmony, and true balance, and somehow I was fortunate enough to be invited inside. I'll never forget that night.

Downhill Kaddish

Frank Cashman

St. Sauveur, Quebec, Canada

My father died ten years ago, in 1993. We had not been close since my parents separated when I was fifteen, but we had regular contact and I had felt somewhat attached to him. I was also in the early stages of "religiosity" and felt an obligation to say Kaddish for him regularly.

Finding a shul where I felt comfortable was difficult for me. I was most at ease with Lubavitch, who had welcomed me ten years before when I was seeking some connection with *Yiddishkeit* and Jewish practice. I was a big-time *am ha'aretz* in the Jewish world, but I was well trained in the secular world holding advanced degrees. I am not sure what drove me — drives me — to religion, but the motivation was there.

My father's death was an awkward situation. He was an independent man and refused my offers of help. When he died, there was a family burial plot in a nearby Jewish community, where there was a large population of Jews. I didn't know anyone there, and there weren't many who knew about my grief or situation. It was a sad scene at the burial — there were not enough people to say Kaddish. In fact, I did not say Kaddish until I returned to Toronto, where I had friends and supportive family. Complicating the situation was the fact our house was being renovated, and I had to sit *shivah* in a close friend's home.

Lubavitch (I use the term to refer to a variety of kind and excellent rabbis) went out of their way to attend the *shivah*, as did my friends. I did not feel comfortable leading the davening — and still don't — but people did it for me.

But the scene at the burial stayed with me — I felt like the community had abandoned me.

Six months later, a rather unusual Kaddish renewed my attachment to *Yiddishkeit*.

I had promised my family a ski trip during the winter break, so we set off for Mount St. Sauveur in Quebec where our friends had a cottage. I knew Kaddish would be a problem since the days ended early and the minyan was thirty minutes away by icy roads. Besides, I did not want to force my children to miss skiing or leave them without a father to watch over them and keep them out of danger.

My friend recognized my difficulty and decided to organize a minyan wherever we were. As it happened, we were at the top of the ski lift one afternoon as the sun set below the horizon and the day came to an end. My friend, being far more connected to his *Yiddishkeit* and less self-conscious than I was, began pulling Jewish males off the lifts as they arrived at the top of the hill. He gathered a minyan of about fifteen skiers, and we stood in our boots, skis, ski caps, goggles, and earmuffs, all facing east. I was not sure if this was proper, but said Kaddish.

In retrospect, this was a meaningful experience, and it was also a memorable place to praise Hashem. I was grateful to my friend who helped me when I needed him.

Toward the evening, I had to daven *minchah*, and I was ready to go to the shul twenty miles away, but again my friend said he would get a minyan together. This time it took place in a large ski lodge with hundreds of gentiles looking at us. I suppose this was also a type of *kiddush Hashem*. At least, I hope it was.

Of my entire year saying Kaddish, these are the minyans that I remember the most.

The Tzaddik of Gaza

Anita Tucker

Netzer Hazani, Gaza

On December 20, 2002, Rabbi Yitzchak Arama, forty, of Netzer Hazani was shot and killed while driving to a prewedding Shabbat celebration in Afula. Islamic Jihad claimed responsibility for the attack. This is a report by a member of his yishuv.

Anita Tucker was known as the grandmother of Gush Katif. She had her own greenhouse, and she was one of the main spokespeople during the disengagement. She was expelled en masse with her moshav, and as of this writing she is still in temporary accommodation.

It was about 10 a.m. Friday morning. Rabbi Arama, his wife Oshrat, and their six children were on their way to Afula to attend the *Shabbat Chatan* celebration for Gilad Yefet, a resident of Netzer Hazani and the brother of Itamar Yefet, who had been killed by terrorist gunfire at the Gush Katif junction in November 2000. A single bullet penetrated the car door and struck Rabbi Arama in the chest as he and his family were approaching the Kissufim Junction entrance to Gush Katif. He died a short while later.

Born in Herzliyah, Yitzchak Arama attended the *hesder* yeshivah in Kiryat Shemona. He received his rabbinical training at Kollel Magal, and seven years before his death he was appointed rabbi of Netzer Hazani and settled there with his family. The entire community was deeply shocked by his death. Rabbi Arama served as an anchor and support for the extended Netzer Hazani family, who had suffered a number of losses to terrorist attacks in the previous two years.

A direct descendant of the fifteenth-century Torah and *Rashi* commentator of the same name, the Akeidat Yitzchak, Rabbi Arama himself was the author of a commentary on *Kohelet*, published in memory of eighteen-year-old Itamar Yefet. Yoram Tzror, local head of security, described Rabbi Arama as the heart and life of the community. He taught Torah not only in his own community, but also throughout Gush Katif. Another resident described him as an "unbelievable combination of the ultimate in humility and Torah knowledge."

The *rav*'s seat in the first row usually sits empty now. No one in the *yishuv* will sit there. Rabbi Arama's oldest son, Matitya, always sat next to that seat and still does, and his younger brother Malachi sits next to him. The *minhag* (custom) in our shul is that people say Kaddish one at a time, not all together at once in one voice. This was also the *minhag* of the Chazon Ish, and it is the way it is done in the Chazon Ish synagogue in Bnei Brak. So Matitya usually has one of the Kaddishes. He has a strong clear voice and pronounces each word of the Aramaic so clearly that I'm sure he understands every one. There is absolute silence in the shul every time Matitya says Kaddish. You can tell that at that moment everyone in the room feels close to their beloved and revered Rav Yitzchak, and you can almost hear Rabbi Arama answering "Amen!"

Malachi, who is younger, is allowed to say Kaddish with his brother. Sometimes he does and sometimes he doesn't, since the Aramaic words are hard for him. However, when both young voices say it together, it melts the hearts of every person there, no matter how tough he is. And hearing those words of praise of HaKadosh Baruch Hu from those two children brings everyone closer to Hashem. The congregation's "Amen" comes out somehow in one clear loud voice, as if one person said "Amen" and not two hundred.

When the custom for each person to say Kaddish separately began in our shul, we were told that it is important that each person who says Kaddish be heard. People have come to accept this gladly and it causes closeness and unity. We have learned to respect each other more as well as respect the laws of precedence in halachah.

One of the adults in our community has a brother with Down syndrome. He is in his thirties or forties and lives with his sister in Jerusalem. Every few months he comes for an extended stay to be with his sister in Netzer Hazani. He is called, affectionately, "Charlie" and is well known by everyone in the moshav. He comes to every prayer service on time and sings along with all the prayers. He is especially diligent in saying every Kaddish.

Although this is not the *minhag* in the shul and Charlie has no obligation, no one has ever protested his saying Kaddish out loud with whoever was given Kaddish that day. When people ask him for whom he is saying Kaddish, he answers confidently, "It's a *chiyuv* — I am obligated to say Kaddish."

One of the young people who stood close to Charlie a few times while he was saying Kaddish said he actually only says the first part accurately. In spite of this, no one has ever complained or objected. When Charlie says Kaddish, everyone has a feeling that this Kaddish reaches very close to the *Kisei HaKavod* (Heavenly Throne). The result is that the congregation's "Amen" has more sincerity and strength than when Charlie is not with us.

A Momentary Crisis of Faith

Rabbi Yechiel Goldreich

Budapest, Hungary

It was 1945. The war had finally ended. But for Yechiel Michel, it was not over. As he emerged from the rubble of Budapest, he proclaimed: "There is no G-d!"

He had lost five children in the Holocaust and only managed to survive the war because he, his wife, and his youngest

Rabbi Yechiel Goldreich is assistant rabbi at Congregation Bnai Torah in Toronto.

child hid as gentiles. They went to church and wore crosses. What other choice did they have?

When Budapest was liberated, Yechiel Michel became angry with G-d. He said to his wife and son that if G-d could allow such a thing as the Holocaust to happen, he wanted no part of his religion.

For an hour he railed against the Almighty: "If until now we lived as gentiles, that is what we'll remain. I want no more part of Judaism!"

The next day, when the family members emerged from their demolished house, his young son noticed him scanning the faces of other survivors. He recognized a few of them as Jews and called them over. Right then and there, he assembled a minyan and led the group in *minchah*.

Amazed, his son asked him, "What about what you said yesterday?"

"That was yesterday " he said. "Today I need to say Kaddish for your siblings!"

It was the last the child ever heard of his father's heresy.

And I am living proof of it. I was named after my *zeide*, Yechiel Michel, who died an observant Jew five years before I was born.

Neither Rain, nor Sleet, nor Blizzards...

Rabbi Asher Herson

Rockaway, New Jersey

In 1996, a blizzard dumped close to three feet of snow in our neck of Rockaway, New Jersey. It was a day to stay at home and wait out the storm. Instead I found myself trekking almost a mile through impassable streets — because of one Jew's commitment to say Kaddish.

This Jew, a man of thirty-five, whose Hebrew name is Shalom Binyamin, had started saying Kaddish a few months before after the passing of his father. Although he had no formal day school education, he undertook to say Kaddish every day. He was the only child, of three, to even consider it. Because of this commitment, he started to come to our Chabad Center every morning and evening without fail!

Before long he started walking to the center every Shabbat from his home, about two miles away. This new level of observance was a direct byproduct of his saying Kaddish for his father.

When the blizzard of '96 hit, there was a travel ban and I didn't even consider making the trek to shul. We live in a rural setting, and I couldn't imagine that anyone would walk the considerable distance in a blizzard. In the early morning hours, I couldn't call and disturb everyone in order to make different plans. I resigned myself to davening at home that day.

As I was preparing to put on my tallit and tefillin, I got a call from the shul. It was my new friend Shalom Binyamin. He wanted to know if we had changed the time of the morning minyan.

It seems that he had trekked the two miles to shul without thinking twice!

Knowing how committed he was to saying Kaddish, and that this was his lifeline to all the other mitzvahs, I told him I would get a minyan together and proceeded to call the regular "minyanaires."

Despite the hour of the morning, everyone I called (make that woke) was amenable, especially knowing that our friend was there, although it would take some time for them all to gear up and walk over. By the time I finished making all the calls and made my own four-fifths-of-a-mile trek in the snow to the Chabad Center, I found that those who had already come were sitting and having a little *farbrengen*, a get-together with lively discussion, in preparation for davening. It made for a very inspirational scene.

The davening was very special, as is any mitzvah that comes with hardship, and afterward we all made our way home. With my friend as inspiration, we returned for *minchah* and *ma'ariv* and even had a class.

Today, Shalom Binyamin still comes to shul every morning and has become an important part of our community.

One departed soul ignited one *neshamah* who in turn ignited many others and continues to do so.

Ten Men and a Touchdown

Max Dekelbaum

Washington, D.C.

My mother, of blessed memory, passed away in February 2001. I was saying Kaddish regularly and was able to plan my work schedule around the times of minyanim.

I own Shalom Kosher Market and Max's Kosher Café in Silver Spring, Maryland. We also have a kosher booth at FedEx Stadium where the Washington Redskins play. The booth is open for most football games that do not take place on

Shabbat or holidays. One time I had no choice but to work at the booth during the time when I would have to daven *minchah* and *ma'ariv*. I was able to ask some friends who I knew would be going to the game to help me out. I also asked men that came up to purchase food to please come back and help make a minyan.

I was very fortunate to have more than ten men return. We were able to daven even though the booth was still open for business and very busy.

The game was quite exciting. The Redskins were playing the New York Giants in a battle of Eastern Conference rivals. As we were finishing praying, we heard the roars and cheers of the entire stadium. The Redskins had just scored a touchdown.

Our joy did not last forever. The Giants defeated the Skins that afternoon. But it was the first time a minyan was ever held at the stadium.

Sixteen Months Kaddish

Rabbi Nachum Kook

Ramat Gan, Israel

In the mid-1980s, there lived a man in my neighborhood who never used to come to synagogue. When he was seventy-three years old, he lost his sister in Romania. She lived in a town where there was no minyan and no Kaddish.

Rabbi Nachum Kook, seventy-five, is the grandson of the brother of Rabbi Avraham HaKohen Kook (1865–1935), the first chief rabbi of Israel. The Kook family boasts many prominent rabbis throughout Israel, including Rabbi Simcha Kook, the chief rabbi of Rechovot.

He started attending shul, putting on tefillin, learning the prayers, and saying Kaddish.

This went on for nine months, then ten months, then twelve months, and on into fourteen months.

There is no law forbidding a person to say Kaddish past the obligatory eleven months after a death, but one is not obligated to do so. After sixteen months, a friend said to him, "You know, you don't have to say Kaddish anymore."

He came to me and said, "I've been saying Kaddish for sixteen months. What is the law?"

When I hear a question, I never answer it right away. I first think, what did he intend by this question? Why would he ask that?

Ten days went by and I still hadn't given him an answer. So he asked again, "What is the law?"

Everyone in the shul waited anxiously for the answer. I looked the man squarely in the eye and told him, "My dear friend, by the letter of the law, you don't have to say Kaddish. However, one thing you must say each day is 'Yehei Shemei rabba mevorach l'olam u'le'olmei olmaya — May His great Name be blessed forever and ever."

He kept coming to shul until he moved to an old age home. This stands out in my mind as one great story of Kaddish.

> *Editor's note: I first heard this story from Rabbi Chanan Yitzchaki, who was a shaliach at the Community Hebrew Academy of Toronto. It truly moved me and I have told it again and again at many shivah houses. Because of it, I try to get to a minyan as often as I can — even if it's difficult to do so and even if I'm late — just so I can also recite that phrase "Yehei Shemei rabba..."*

Kaddish for Ilan

Rabbi Tzvi Konikov

Satellite Beach, Florida

Ilan Ramon was only forty-eight years old when he was killed in the space shuttle disaster, on the twenty-ninth of Shevat, February 1, 2003. He embraced and represented all Jews when he took with him a sefer Torah and a dollar from the Lubavitcher Rebbe, made Kiddush, and said the Shema Yisrael in orbit. Here is the story as told by his rabbi, Rabbi Tzvi Konikov of Chabad Satellite Beach.

The morning of liftoff was Thursday, January 16, 2003. That morning we were all invited to watch the launch: family from Israel, Israel Air Force personnel, and the media. We passed through the tightest security I've ever seen in my life — snipers on roofs, canine dogs, and police in full gear. Hundreds of Israelis and VIP's came to watch the launch. I didn't want to miss it for anything, but I was in a predicament: I had to say Kaddish for my mother, who had passed away that year.

I invited six other rabbis to watch the liftoff to ensure that we would have a minyan. Israeli radio, television, and press all witnessed another great liftoff: our minyan! Many Israelis joined in. I didn't have enough tefillin for everyone.

One lady asked, "Are you making a service to pray for the astronauts to have a safe trip?"

I replied, "Absolutely!"

Two Israeli rabbis from South Florida helped translate the countdown and liftoff into Hebrew. It brought tears to my eyes.

On Shabbat, February 1, we heard immediately about the shuttle crash. I told Rona, Ilan's wife, that I wanted to be with the family. I made plans right away to attend the funeral in Israel. As I stopped in New York Sunday morning at the airport, my dad immediately handed me my ticket for Israel. As divine providence would have it, the *aron* (coffin) with Ilan's body was on the same plane with us. His was the only body of all the astronauts that was found and was recognizable. An honor guard of U.S. soldiers stood guard by the coffin. Israeli army officers and the *rav* of the Israel Defense Forces accompanied them.

As I said the Kaddish on the plane, I felt I was saying it twofold: for my mom, but also for Ilan. The entire plane was brought to tears. One stewardess promised to light Shabbat candles from then on in memory of Ilan. I saw firsthand how the mitzvah of Kaddish leads to other mitzvot.

At the *shivah* in Holon, I recited Kaddish along with the father and son of Ilan. I was the only rabbi there throughout the entire *shivah* period.

Ilan will never be forgotten.

Executive Chesed

Yisroel Idels

Los Angeles, California

My mother and father moved from Miami, where my brother and I grew up, to Leisure World, a retirement community in Southern California, to be closer to family. They lived there for more than twenty happy years, while my wife and I were raising our family in Toronto. A year after my parents moved from Leisure World to a seniors' residence in Los Angeles, my mother passed away. The family decided to have the unveiling in August, shortly before the end of the first year of mourning.

Having scheduled the unveiling for a Tuesday afternoon, and not knowing people in the Los Angeles Orthodox community, it seemed that there would be just four men present at the cemetery, including my father, brother, and nephew.

We had arrived in Los Angeles on Sunday. By Tuesday morning davening, I was a bit upset that no one in the shul had recognized a stranger in their midst. Immediately, I reminded myself of the *mishnah* in *Pirkei Avot*, "*Hevei dan et kol adam l'chaf zechut* — Judge people on the scale of merit." I thought to myself, *They're preoccupied. They just haven't noticed.*

No more than a few minutes passed when suddenly a group of daveners approached me with a "*Shalom aleichem!* Where are you from?" One of my greeters, who introduced himself as Ralph Rubenstein, was delighted to hear that I was from Toronto, where he had grown up.

Leaving the shul much happier, I decided to look for a place to grab a quick breakfast. Entering a local bakery, I was surprised to see that the only other patron was Ralph! Again he greeted me warmly and asked me about the purpose of my trip.

I explained that my mother's unveiling was scheduled for four o'clock that afternoon. He asked if I would have a minyan. I said we wouldn't because we didn't really know anyone in the city.

When he heard that, he said, "Please, I'll make a few phone calls, and maybe we can get a minyan for you."

"But it's such short notice. It's in the middle of a workday, and the cemetery is an easy forty-five minutes away."

Ralph, though, was not to be put off. He asked for my cell phone number with the hope of getting back to me.

The morning passed quickly since I was involved with many family matters. Hours later my cell phone rang.

"Hello, this is Ralph. I've got nine men. We'll see you this afternoon."

We arrived at the cemetery to see three cars of complete strangers waiting for us. Their presence infused the unveiling with meaning and emotion. We recited psalms, I was able to eulogize my mother, and a tearful Kaddish was said by father and sons.

Deeply grateful, we said "thank you" to those who had come. Out of curiosity, I asked the younger men, as they were getting into a car, what their occupation was. I was deeply touched when they told me they worked for Ralph.

An executive had interrupted a busy day, bringing employees, family, and friends, to allow fellow Jews — and perfect strangers — to say Kaddish for a mother whose soul was immeasurably elevated by the love and concern of one Jew to another.

Mission Accomplished!

Rabbi Gedalia Zweig

Chicago, Illinois

One of my more memorable Kaddish stories happened the day we were coming back from our vacation in Orlando.

In February 2002, I had made reservations for a week in Miami and a week in Orlando for the following December. (After September 11, many people postponed their vacations and canceled flights, so I took no chances and booked early.)

When my mother died a few weeks later, on March 1, 2002, in the back of my mind I thought of Kaddish. But we were going to be in Miami and Orlando, both cities with a large population of Jews. Surely I would have no problem finding a minyan.

It was on the way home that I had the problem. We had bought the ticket using air miles points, and we were limited in the flights we could book. Our return flight left Orlando at 7 a.m. and it would be stopping in Chicago. I knew I might have a problem finding a minyan to say Kaddish.

As it happened, the previous summer I had met a young couple from Chicago at a kosher bakery in Toronto. I helped them with directions. I thought maybe they could help me in turn.

"By the way, I will be stopping in Chicago at O'Hare Airport and I need to find a minyan nearby. What can I do?"

The husband gave me a few options. I could take a cab to Skokie Yeshivah (about a twenty-five-minute ride) and say Kaddish with the boys there, or I could go to the local Chabad House and get a minyan, although it didn't have a regular service. No good.

But what do you know — there was a morning minyan twenty minutes away from the airport, and it happened to be the latest one in Chicago: 9 a.m. at FREE (the Federation of Refugees of Eastern Europe) on Devon. So that became the plan: stop over at O'Hare, go to minyan, and return to the airport to board the plane for Toronto.

When the plane touched down early at 8:35 a.m. Central Time (I gained an hour coming from Orlando in the Eastern Time zone), I looked over my equipment as if I were James Bond: tefillin — check; boarding pass — check; directions — check!

I hailed the first cab I saw, optimistic on two counts: the driver spoke English and it was a clear day. We arrived shortly after 9 a.m.

I told the driver to wait in front, that I'd only be a half-hour and I'd pay for his time. So far, so good!

But guess what — that day it happened that we had the slowest chazzan in town!

He crawled through the prayers and Torah reading. When we reached the *MiShebeirach* prayers (for the sick) I finally interjected.

"I am really sorry, but could we just go a little faster? I really do have a plane to catch!"

We finally finished, and I was able to recite all my Kaddishes.

Beautiful city, Chicago, I said to myself as we headed back to the airport.

I entered the terminal again and went through security. More checking. We sat down at our seat with moments to spare.

My wife and son turned to me and smiled. Kaddish recited. Mission accomplished!

In-Flight Kaddish

Yosi Heber

London, England

Reb Yosi Heber is a successful businessman in Detroit. In 1996 he was saying Kaddish for his father and traveled overseas many times. He went on twenty-four flights during this period. Only once was the plane late. But guess what? Because it was late, he was able to daven with a minyan. Here is a great "in-flight" Kaddish story.

Yosi had his whole schedule worked out. He was off to visit England, where he and his wife had lived many years earlier. And he was not about to miss a Kaddish.

On the way home, he caught the 6:30 a.m. minyan in London and was leaving via Heathrow, England's largest and busiest airport. His flight was to leave about 1 p.m. and arrive in Israel about 5 p.m., after the time for *minchah*.

How hard can it be to get a minyan on a flight to Israel? he thought to himself.

But as he boarded, he saw only two other *kippot*. He followed the stewardess and saw where she dropped the other kosher meals. Five more people. Then he saw a fellow reading a Hebrew newspaper. Including him, there were now at least nine.

Everyone had dinner and the number stayed at nine for two hours. He wracked his brain.

Where can I find a tenth?

Then he noticed a fellow seated opposite him who looked Jewish. He started chatting with him and twenty-five minutes later asked, "Are you Jewish?"

The fellow responded, "Of course!"

Yosi said, "I need to ask you a big favor. I have to say a prayer for my father, the Kaddish prayer, and I can only say it with ten men. Would you be our tenth?"

The man got teary-eyed and said, "I am forty-five years old. The last time I was in shul was when I was six years old with my dad. And it was to recite a memorial prayer for his dad. Of course I'll help you out. When do we start?"

Lost in the Synagogue

Steve Eigen

I was raised Orthodox, then strayed in my teens and early twenties. My father passed away when I was twenty-eight. I was not a member of any particular congregation, having recently moved to a new area. I selected a synagogue from the phone book and went there to say Kaddish a few hours after returning home from the funeral.

When I walked into the synagogue, I felt so lost I didn't even know which siddur to use. I was so distraught that for a moment I was even having trouble reading Hebrew. The services ended with the Mourner's Kaddish, for which I stood and read aloud. I read the Hebrew much slower than the others in the congregation due to my lack of experience and state of distress. By the time I was finished, I was standing alone in a cold empty synagogue. Not one person came over to me, nor did anyone slow down so I could recite Kaddish along with everyone else. Once I was done, I sat down and cried. I went home and told my family that I would never step foot in a synagogue again.

Luckily, a person paying a *shivah* call recommended I try the synagogue down the road, where he assured me I would have a much different experience. Out of respect for how devoted my father was to his Jewishness and prayers, I agreed.

Sure enough, I had a completely different experience. One person handed me a phonetic prayer book. Someone else handed me a prayer book with an English translation. I explained that I could read Hebrew, but I was just a little rusty and that I had never said Kaddish before. The cantor came down from the *bimah* and stood behind me so that as he led the Mourner's Kaddish he could make sure he didn't go too fast.

Many Jews come to synagogue for the first time in a long while for the express purpose of saying the Mourner's Kaddish. Regular worshipers attend synagogue with greater vigor when they need to say the Mourner's Kaddish. Reflecting upon the death of a deceased loved one is an emotional time. After my experience I realized that it is important that congregations make saying the Mourner's Kaddish as accessible as possible. Here are four suggestions for helping ease this difficult time:

1. *Slow down.* The Mourner's Kaddish should be recited at the pace of the slowest Hebrew reader in the synagogue. This will ensure that everyone has the opportunity to re-

cite the prayer in a comfortable and proper manner.

2. *Announce the page number.* Before reciting the Mourner's Kaddish, announce the page number so that those not familiar with the order of the service or the prayer book will be prepared.

3. *Make copies.* Have copies of the Mourner's Kaddish written out phonetically for those who cannot read Hebrew and in large print for those with vision problems. These copies should be kept next to the prayer books so everyone can help themselves without feeling embarrassed.

4. *Make everyone feel welcome.* Go out of your way to make a newcomer feel welcome. Introduce yourself — if there is a *kiddush* after services, invite the newcomer to attend. Perhaps a member of the minyan committee should take on this responsibility as the official welcoming officer.

A warm and comfortable experience during an emotional time should lead to a greater connection to one's Jewishness and, hopefully, a more observant Jew. It did for me.

I Don't Know about Idaho

Rabbi Dovid Heber

Idaho City, Idaho

I work for the Star-K kosher certification company in Baltimore. My work takes me to various destinations across the United States, including many locations without a functioning minyan.

In November 1996, I was in the year of mourning for my father, Rav Shmuel, a rebbe and chazzan in St. Louis for more than forty years. He served as chazzan on the High Holidays in such far-off places as Russia, Rome, and Argentina. During that year, I had to travel to Idaho Falls, Idaho, to visit a factory. The closest minyan in any direction was more than four hundred miles away. What would I do for a minyan to say Kaddish?

After much research, I located a Jewish man who said he would make some phone calls. There was also a Jewish fellow from Big Sky, Montana, whom I now learn with on the phone. His name is Paul Pariser, and he drove 150 miles, mostly on two-lane roads, to help form the minyan. He was accompanied by the Big Sky doctor and his son, who were also Jewish.

On Thursday, November 7, 1996, we formed a minyan late one afternoon at the home of Mr. and Mrs. Saul Mandel on Malibu Drive. I delivered a brief class following *ma'ariv*. I was so excited about the Torah learning among the participants that I got to the airport only five minutes before the scheduled departure of my flight that evening.

One advantage of being in such a small airport is the ability to make it from the front door to the flight in two minutes. A disadvantage is that flights leave early! My flight was pulling away as I ran toward the gate!

I wondered how I would make it back to Baltimore for Shabbat, let alone in time for *shacharit*.

Fortunately there was one more connecting flight to Salt Lake City that allowed me to catch my red eye flight back east in time for the late Friday morning *shacharit* in Baltimore.

This was a tremendous merit for my father, who himself had gone to far-flung places in order to lead a minyan.

Kaddish for Baby Yehuda

Benni Shoham

Shilo, Israel

My name is Benni Shoham and I live in the *yishuv* of Shilo, the ancient capital of Israel where the first Mishkan was located for 369 years.

We have seen our share of terrorism during the Oslo War. My son Yehuda has the distinction of being the youngest terror victim during that time. He was a mere five months old when he was taken from us.

On the evening of June 5, 2001, my wife, Batsheva, and I were passing by the Arab village of Luban a-Sharkiya when young Arabs started hurling stones at our car. Our young son Yehuda was fast asleep in the back seat. A ten-pound stone crashed through the windshield. Passing between my wife and me, it hit the back seat and rebounded into Yehuda.

He was rushed to the Hadassah Hospital intensive care unit. He never regained consciousness. His brain had ceased to function, and only a respirator and prayers were sustaining him.

For six days, we stood by our son's bedside, keeping vigil. Streams of people from all walks of life visited, phoned, and prayed. Prime Minister Ariel Sharon joined us at Yehuda's bedside to read psalms.

Yehuda died on June 1. His funeral procession began at the prime minister's residence in Jerusalem, then left the city and headed toward Shilo. There, the residents stood tearfully along the roadside to meet the procession. Though they had witnessed the horror of terrorism many times, their eyes were filled with sadness at the death of one so young.

I think the strongest feelings I had were when I said Kaddish with my son in front of me just before he was buried. Every word had deep meaning — and in moments like that, you think about every word. I remember thinking that this was G-d's will and that we needed to go on with our lives, as hard as this would be.

In those early days we kept asking ourselves why this had happened to us. We went to see four different chief rabbis of various communities. They gave us a lot of strength and blessed us, saying that we needed to be strong and that we should continue to build our family, *b'ezrat Hashem*.

We have a strong *emunah* and we are going forward! Everything we do today is in memory of our son. Always be strong and know that G-d is with you.

Editor's note: Since my meeting with Benni Shoham, much good has happened. The Gemara says if one has a child after losing one, the pain is healed. About one year after Yehuda's death, Benni was blessed with a son. He was also blessed with a daughter in early April 2004 and another son in October 2005. He lectures in Israel and around the Jewish world, often at seminars for families of terror victims. Benni's message is one of love, belief, and patience with the Almighty.

The Tenth Man

Sara Karmely

Santa Barbara, California

The Ba'al Shem Tov taught that every Jew is as dear to Hashem as an only child born to a couple in their old age. How the Holy One nurtures His children is evident, and it is so touching to see how they respond, in their simple sincerity. No Jew ever slips through the cracks, although sometimes he or she returns late in life.

Recently, there was a *Shabbaton* on the Channel Islands near Santa Barbara, California. It included a group of young Iranian singles who had formed a little organization called

This story is reprinted with permission from the N'shei Chabad newsletter.

Roots. Their goal was to inspire others to become *shomer mitzvot*. Rabbi Dovid Loloyan and his worthy *rebbetzin*, Ronit, would be speaking and so would I.

The group consisted mostly of young women, but we should have had enough men for a minyan. To our dismay, some of the boys who had made a commitment to come did not make it, and we had only nine men. This posed a problem for Rabbi Loloyan, who had to say Kaddish for his father who had recently passed away.

Friday night after candle lighting found the whole group waiting around, unable to start the Shabbat davening. The mood was gloomy. Finally, I commented that obviously this was all Hashem's plan. This was happening in order to get us to look for a Jew who was right now in our hotel, a Jew who would not otherwise be going to daven. We sent a couple of the boys down to the lobby to inquire at the front desk.

"Excuse me, do you happen to know if there are any Jews booked into your hotel?" they asked hopefully.

"*Che?*" responded the man behind the desk. It was quite obvious that he did not understand what they wanted. They asked to look at the register to check for themselves if there were any Jewish names, but the clerk would not permit it.

Just as they were about to give up, one of the boys, who was wearing a *kippah*, felt someone clap a hand on his shoulder and heard a welcome, "*Gut Shabbos*!" He spun around to see a smiling elderly man wearing shorts and a T-shirt.

"Are you Jewish?" the boy asked excitedly.

"Yes, I am," was the answer.

Immediately, the call went out: "We found a Jew!"

The other men from our group came running and, without further ado, carried off a surprised (and amused) Mr. Rosen.

His name happened to be Eliyahu, and they joked, "You must be Eliyahu HaNavi sent to us because we need a tenth man!"

The joy at that Shabbat davening was almost palpable. They had a minyan! Hashem had helped them! Rabbi Loloyan could say Kaddish!

After *Lechah Dodi*, the men and boys lifted Mr. Rosen onto their shoulders and danced around the *bimah* with him. Then they carefully guided their new friend through the davening, teaching him when to stand and bow.

He told everyone, "This is the first time I can actually understand what I'm praying."

He had never had such a Shabbat. He grew up belonging to a Reform temple. But he remembered, as a boy, his father and grandfather being religious.

After davening, we invited Mr. Rosen downstairs to share in our Shabbat meal. At first he demurred, but after some persuading he relented. He thoroughly enjoyed every aspect of the *seudah*, dutifully washing for bread (coached by the boys). But most of all, he was inspired by Rabbi Loloyan's brilliant, scholarly speeches, which he found quite interesting and illuminating. He even joined in the *zemirot* (Shabbat songs), humming along, because although he did not know the words, clearly his *neshamah* knew the tunes.

Finally, the long, beautiful Friday night was over, and we asked Mr. Rosen to please come to our shul in the morning. He was our tenth man, and without him we could not read from the Torah.

"Sorry, don't count on me," he said firmly. "I really can't come. I have to leave early in the morning."

Our disappointed pleas fell on deaf ears. Although he was deeply moved by the taste of Shabbat that he had just experienced, Mr. Rosen had his plans and would not change them.

Well, what do you know, the first one to come to the minyan on Shabbat morning was none other than Mr. Rosen! He was waiting impatiently for the rest of us to come. He told us that he had not been able to sleep. He had felt very touched by the way the boys obviously loved davening, and he wanted to be a part of it again. We knew that this Jew's *pintele Yid* (Jewish spark) had been rekindled, and it would give him no rest until it was allowed to burst into full flame.

Rabbi Loloyan made sure that our guest got an *aliyah*, after which the boys again carried him aloft, dancing around the *bimah* with him, to his great glee. It was like seeing this man, who was at least in his mid-seventies, become young again. You could not help but get choked up when you looked at his beaming, happy face and saw the *ahavat Yisrael* (love of fellow Jews) that the boys showed him.

It says in *Devarim* (30:1–10): "If your outcasts be at the ends of the heavens, from there will G-d gather you, from there He will take you."

Eliyahu Rosen is no longer an outcast from the Jewish people — Rabbi Loloyan will make sure that he is now included among his people. As the Rebbe said many times, no Jew is far away. He just needs to be drawn nearer.

A Second Chance at Kaddish

Menachem Rosenblum

Brooklyn, New York

Being the only son in my family, when my father passed away in Jerusalem, I made a solemn resolution to be the chazzan and say Kaddish three times a day throughout my year of mourning. Though it was no easy feat to find a minyan three times a day that would allow me to be the chazzan, I managed to find various ways of improvising so as to honor my father and the pledge I had made.

Every evening I would work out where I would daven the following day so I would be able to be a chazzan for all three *tefillah* services. At times I would arrive at a minyan only to find that someone else had a *chiyuv* for a *yahrtzeit* and took precedence over me. Luckily, living in Brooklyn, there is no shortage of shuls — it was just a matter of finding one that would allow me to be chazzan.

At the time, I owned a flower shop in Boro Park. Part of my work was doing flower arrangements for weddings and other *simchah*s. On nights that I had to work late and couldn't get out of the shop, I would hire yeshivah students to come to my shop and make up a minyan so I could be chazzan.

There isn't a *nusach* (prayer style) I didn't daven that year — all so I could be chazzan and say Kaddish with a minyan. It was a period in my life when I was building up my business, working long hours, and often traveling around New York City to various wedding halls to set up the flower arrangements. I had to coordinate my hectic schedule with a wide variety of shuls located in various locations. A good portion of my day was preoccupied with where I was going to catch the next minyan where I could be chazzan and recite Kaddish.

Throughout that year, I never missed a minyan, and I always managed to be the chazzan. It was by far the most difficult thing I had ever undertaken, but it was one I fulfilled out of honor and respect for my father, who had been exacting and meticulous about halachah and never allowed any obstacles to stand in his way. Then, with only one month to go until the end of the year of mourning, I nearly broke what had been up to then a perfect record.

Through our frequent trips to Israel, we had accumulated enough mileage for a free trip to Israel that summer that would include most of my family. But "free" also meant inconvenient flight connections. We'd have to travel first to Paris and from there catch a flight to Israel. My wife and I and five of our children boarded a plane to Paris at 8 p.m. *Ma'ariv* at that time of year was at 9:30.

After boarding the plane, I walked slowly through the aisles, carefully scrutinizing the passengers, searching for *kippot, shtreimels*, fedora hats, and even baseball caps. I needed to get a minyan together and nobody looked even remotely Jewish. I couldn't believe that the year was almost over and of all situations — being on the way to Israel to visit my widowed mother — I wasn't going to be able to get together a minyan to say Kaddish. With a heavy heart, I called a close friend of mine on my cell phone and asked him to say Kaddish at *ma'ariv*, giving him my father's name, just in case I wouldn't succeed in davening *ma'ariv* with a minyan that night.

The plane took off. It was about 10:30 when the seatbelt lights turned off. My wife, Faige, and I went around the plane asking each man whether he was Jewish. Every time I got an answer in the affirmative, I asked that person to please join me for *ma'ariv* services at the back of the plane. Nobody was interested.

We tried another tactic. We went around again saying that I had to say Kaddish, so would they please join me at the back of the plane for *ma'ariv* services? After much effort and persuasion, we were finally able to get nine Jewish men (including passengers from business class and first class) to reluctantly agree to do me the enormous favor of making up a minyan so that I could say Kaddish. By the time we were able to get them together, dinner was being served and everyone had to sit down. After dinner, we went back to the nine men who had given their consent to make up a minyan, but now, after having eaten, they were tired, and one by one they backed out. I was left with only five men who were willing to help me out with a minyan. Greatly disheartened, I returned to my seat, dejected and depressed.

I had just returned to my seat when the plane suddenly encountered wild turbulence. We're seasoned air travelers, but we had never experienced anything like this. The dinner trays went flying in every direction, and the overhead compartments flew open, with bags and suitcases spilling out into the aisles and onto the heads of the passengers. There was screaming and crying everywhere. My wife turned to me and said, "I guess you won't have to worry about Kaddish anymore." She told the children to hold hands, and together we recited the Shema. We really thought we were going to die.

After about four or five minutes — though it seemed like an eternity — just as suddenly as it started, the turbulence ended, the plane stabilized, and everything returned to normal.

The captain made an announcement over the loudspeaker saying that he had been flying planes for more than twenty-five years and this was the worst turbulence he had ever experienced.

Immediately following this frightening experience, my wife went over to the flight attendant and asked her to announce that evening services followed by Kaddish would be recited in the next few minutes at the back of the plane. Within moments, the aisles were filled with men — lots of men — making their way to the back of the plane. By the time I got there, there were more than fifty men waiting for me to begin the service.

Faige asked the flight attendant for a bunch of napkins for their heads, since not one of them owned a head covering. Together with the kids, my wife distributed the TWA napkins that served as *kippot*.

Since no one had a siddur, I instructed the group to say "Amen" every time I raised my hand. I also instructed them to recite the Shema after me word for word. *Ma'ariv* was conducted with the 100 percent cooperation of willing Jewish passengers who heartily answered "Amen" to my raised hand and recited the Shema, probably for the first time since their bar mitzvahs.

My father's Kaddish was answered "*b'rov am*" in the most dignified and respectable way imaginable. This filled me with the indescribable satisfaction that I had fulfilled the mitzvah of honoring my father's memory to the utmost degree.

Kaddish at JFK

Rabbi Ari Styner

New York, New York

I was waiting to board a flight at New York's John F. Kennedy International Airport when my plane was suddenly delayed. I began wandering around the terminal when a bearded man asked me to make a minyan because he had a *yahrtzeit*. So far I was the only other person in his minyan. I agreed to help him recruit eight others.

After twenty minutes, we had gathered several *kippah*-wearing men and a few in baseball caps who were also Jewish. But with only eight people in total, we were about to give up and return to our gates. Then I heard a couple speaking Hebrew in a corner. The man was a secular Israeli. I explained the situation and he was willing to join us.

We were still one man short, and we were all losing patience. Our flights would be leaving shortly and so we didn't have much time.

Suddenly an announcement came over the public address system saying that due to the weather, all flights would be grounded for one more hour. Within minutes, we found another Jew, an older man. We started shmoozing, and he said he would join us, but he would not daven.

I asked what had brought him to New York City. He replied that his sister had died three days earlier and that he was done sitting *shivah*.

I tried to talk him into continuing to say Kaddish, but he refused. He changed the subject, asking where I was from. I told him I lived in Des Moines, Iowa.

His eyes grew wide. "Do you know David Bassman?" he asked.

"Of course," I said. "He comes to my shul every day. But how do you know him?"

"We're neighbors in Florida and very good friends."

We chatted about Dave's commitment to davening with a minyan. By the time we were done talking, we had our minyan and were about to daven.

At that point, the man said, "You know, I enjoyed talking with you, Rabbi. Do you think you can help me say Kaddish for my sister?"

And so, right there in JFK Airport two men said the Mourner's Kaddish together, and the souls of their loved ones looked down from Heaven and smiled.

Remembrance at the Kotel

Michoel Yonasan Sender

Jerusalem, Israel

My mother died in January 1983. For ten years, no one said Kaddish for her. When I became religious a decade after her death, I learned of my obligation to say Kaddish on her *yahrtzeit*. I came to Israel at that time to learn in a yeshivah and was excited that I had the opportunity to say my first Kaddish for my mother at the Kotel.

I arrived in February 1993. I knew my mother's *yahrtzeit* was some time at the end of the year, but I didn't look up the exact date. Later that year I was fortunate enough to become a *chatan* (bridegroom), and with all the whirlwind of activity, I forgot about my mother's *yahrtzeit*.

On the twentieth of Tevet, January 1994, there was a day of prayer at the Kotel due to the difficult situation in Israel. *Gedolei Torah* and all the yeshivot went, including mine. The *New York Times* reported that 20,000 people were there, but everyone present knew there were a lot more. There was so little space that many people went on rooftops to participate. Tens of thousands of Jews said *Tehillim* together and then davened *minchah*.

As the sun was setting, a feeling of dread came over me like I never had before. I realized I had forgotten about my mother's *yahrtzeit* and it might have even passed. I was standing next to my *rosh yeshivah*, and I told him what happened. We davened *ma'ariv* and rushed back to his house where he had a book that could help us determine the Hebrew date of my mother's *yahrtzeit*.

As he was looking it up, I wanted to confirm with my family the time of my mother's death because I knew it was around sunset. In fact, I knew my mother died at about 5 p.m., because I was alone in the hospital room with her. But after ten years, I wanted to confirm this information. I called my sister, but she wasn't home. I reached my father, though, and he confirmed it was at 5 p.m. As I was speaking to him, my rabbi brought the book over and told me that January 5, 1983, was the twentieth of Tevet. It was that very day! We then went to another book to confirm that 5 p.m. in Philadelphia was before sunset, as I had thought. I ran down to the Kotel immediately and joined a *ma'ariv* in time for Kaddish and was able to daven *shacharit* and *minchah* the next day in my mother's *zechut*.

Kaddish in the Camps

Moshe Kraus

Bohr, Yugoslavia

I have been a *sheliach tzibbur* since the age of thirteen — more than sixty-five years. During the Holocaust, I spent a few years in a labor camp in Bohr, Yugoslavia. In 1943, the inmates were able to organize davening for Yom Kippur. I was their chazzan.

That night I began to chant the Kol Nidrei, to the joy of the inmates. At that moment, the SS guards stormed in. They beat the prisoners who were present and took me away. As a punishment, they hung me with my hands tied behind my back for eight hours, then threw me into a cell. They gave me food, but I could not eat since I couldn't move my hands. Amazingly some prisoners found me and fed me.

Later the camp commandant — his name was Kramer — saw me and asked in German, "*Kraus, di liebst noch?*" (Kraus, you're still alive?)

Soon after I was transferred to other concentration camps, including Bergen-Belsen. I recall there was a learned man there, Shmuel Weintraub, who taught the *Daf Yomi* (the daily Talmud section) from memory.

We weren't allowed to daven in those camps. But on occasion someone would remember a *yahrtzeit,* and in the barracks we would say *Aleinu* and the Mourner's Kaddish with ten Jews.

There was a fellow in the camp whose grandfather had converted from Judaism and married a gentile woman. His father, of course, married a non-Jewish woman, and this man grew up as a non-Jew.

Then Hitler came along with the Nuremberg Laws. Even with one Jewish grandparent, a person was considered Jewish. The man would often tell the guards and commandant, "But I'm not even Jewish!"

They didn't care and he received the same treatment as us. After surviving the war, he said, "If G-d spared me as a Jew, I must learn more about this heritage." He learned Hebrew, moved to Israel, and converted to Judaism. He became a Torah scholar, got married, and lives in Meah Shearim. He is now a well-known rabbi in Israel.

Morning at the Minsk

Rabbi Gedalia Zweig

Toronto, Canada

Fifty-five-year-old Beryl Konan is from Nizhny Novgorad, about 400 kilometers (250 miles) east of Moscow. He is fifty-five years old. The city had about 15,000 Jews before the war. He left in 1970. In the old Soviet Union, he never had a chance to experience services in a synagogue. He never had a bar mitzvah, and he never had the chance to say Kaddish. Now, in Toronto, he was saying Kaddish for his mother at Congregation Anshei Minsk, in downtown Toronto.

Friday, April 15, 2005, was like most other Fridays when it comes to trying to put together a minyan at Congregation Anshei Minsk, in the heart of Toronto's bustling Kensington Market.

Once the center of Jewish life in the city, the market is now a multi-ethnic mix of food shops and hip restaurants and clubs. Since the 1980s, the Anshei Minsk — which is often called the Minsker Shul, or just "the Minsk" — has been downtown Toronto's only shul with daily prayer services. The area's Jewish community is now made up of older Jews who chose not to follow the larger community's move north on Bathurst Street, Jewish students and young professionals who prefer downtown to the suburbs, and Jews who have moved into the growing number of condominium developments on Toronto's lakefront. The Minsk also serves Jews who live up north but work downtown and people visiting the sick in one of the many nearby hospitals, as well as tourists and business travelers staying in downtown hotels.

Rabbi Shmuel Spero, spiritual leader of the Minsk since 1988, is a master at gathering ten men so that people who need to can say Kaddish in the heart of Canada's largest city. Lately, it's been Beryl Konan, a Russian immigrant who lives downtown, who has needed a minyan to say Kaddish for his mother. On this Friday, as is the case every weekday, the morning minyan was called for 7:30.

He was running late on this particular day and only got to the shul by 8:20, where he was met by only five people. Since my paint shop is nearby, I got a call on my cell phone from Rabbi Spero at 8:30 to come on down. By 8:45, more than an hour after services were supposed to start, we had only eight men.

"Mike" was in the kitchen and "davening" — well, make that singing some prayers — but he's not Jewish, so we couldn't count him for the minyan. We called Joe Heller, a downtowner from way back whose seventy-five-year-old printing press at 373 Spadina Avenue may well be the oldest surviving business in the area.

We now had nine, but we needed our tenth.

As they hung around and waited, a guy I know only as Harvey played guitar, while old Johnny *shuckled* away and struck a chord on the piano. Rabbi Spero called another semi-regular, Pesach, but he said he couldn't make it for another twenty minutes.

It was 9:15 and we were getting antsy. Finally Rabbi Spero called Daniel the *kohen* on his cell phone. He turned out to be right around the corner. Finally we had our ten men. Meanwhile, two more guys, Oded and Yaniv, rolled in off the street so they could put on tefillin. Also in the minyan was Stefan the cook, sixty-four, a Hungarian Holocaust survivor.

Things were running more than a bit late, but Rabbi Spero had a plan for just what to do in such situations. First we said a short Amidah so we could answer Kedushah together. We called out the day, "*Hayom yom shishi...*" followed by Beryl saying Kaddish, then we said *Ein K'Elokeinu* and *Aleinu*, and we finished up with a loud *Barchu*.

By the time we had breakfast — a key social aspect of the minyan for many of the guys — it was 9:40.

Doesn't anyone work around here? I thought to myself as I got ready to head back to the store. Well, I guess you could say that making a minyan at the Minsk sure is work, and it gave Beryl his opportunity to say Kaddish.

Kaddish with Oprah

Simcha Jacobovici

Chicago, Illinois

The phone rang in my New York hotel room. It was 1995, and I was saying Kaddish for my late father, of blessed memory, Joseph Jacobovici. I live in Toronto, but I'm a filmmaker, so I move around.

During my eleven months of saying Kaddish, I ended up in various minyans from San Francisco to Halifax. Once, I found

Simcha Jacobovici is a two-time Emmy-award-winning filmmaker. His many films include *Falasha: Exile of the Black Jews, Deadly Currents, Quest for the Lost Tribes*, and *Hollywoodism: Jews, Movies and the American Dream*. An Israeli-born Canadian, he is married and the father of four girls and a boy.

myself in a Satmar summer retreat, in Colorado I believe. An-other time, I extended a stopover in Detroit and rushed to the basement of an old shul, where I was greeted by nine octoge-narians as if I were the Messiah himself. But the phone call in New York was the start of what turned out to be perhaps the most interesting Kaddish experience of them all.

I had just finished a documentary film called *The Selling of Innocents*. The film won an Emmy, attracting the attention of Oprah Winfrey, the American icon and celebrated TV host.

The producer at the other end of the telephone line asked if I could fly to Chicago and appear with my fellow producers on the *Oprah* show the day after next.

I was taken aback. This was the *Oprah* show. The big time. Great publicity for the film, and great promotion for me and my company.

"I'd love to do it," I said, "but I don't think I can."

"Why not?" the producer asked, her voice betraying her surprise. Nobody says "too busy" to the *Oprah* show.

"I have a problem," I answered.

The producer's voice, Lisa was her name, became steely. All business. "What's the problem?" she asked.

"It's complicated."

"Try me," she said.

I began the process of explaining to a gentile, female tele-vision producer from Chicago about the Jewish ritual of Kaddish.

Whenever I had to explain this to a secular Jewish organi-zation, they never quite got it. I would tell them that I need a minyan, and they would drive me to an empty shul. I would tell them that I'm Orthodox, and I would find myself in an all-female minyan. It never quite worked out. But this was *Oprah*.

So I gave it a try.

"I'm Jewish. I'm Orthodox. My father passed away. In our religion it's incumbent on me, three times a day, to say a certain prayer, a glorification of G-d's Name, really. It's called Mourner's Kaddish. To do this, I need to be in a 'Jewish quorum.' It's called a minyan. For the Orthodox, this means ten Jewish men. So I can't miss this ritual. If I come to Chicago, I would have to attend morning services prior to being on *Oprah*."

"No problem," she said. "You need a minyan to say Kaddish. Ten Orthodox Jewish men. For morning services. I'll arrange it."

"It's not so simple," I said. "You may find an Orthodox synagogue, but it might not have a minyan in the morning. Or the Jewish community may send you to a synagogue that's open, but is Conservative. They may count women in their minyan, which wouldn't do the trick for me."

Lisa tried to be patient. "I'll fax your flight information to your hotel. You will be met in Chicago by a limo. The driver will have the minyan information. You will say Kaddish for your father."

The rest unfolded like a military operation. The next day the ticket came. Then the limo came. The driver took me to a hotel and said, "I'll be here at 6:30 a.m. Your minyan begins at 7 a.m. I'll pick you up at 8 a.m. You'll be at the *Oprah* show by 8:30 a.m."

The hotel room was beautiful. I slept like a baby.

At 6:30 in the morning, I came down and stepped into my limo. There was a newspaper on the seat.

I could get used to this, I thought.

The driver pulled up in front of a downtown office building

and told me that there was a Chabad Lubavitch minyan on one of the upper floors.

When I got there, the rabbi looked at me and said, "So you're the guy saying Kaddish. I was warned by the *Oprah* show that I'd better have a minyan."

We smiled at each other. I was really impressed with Lisa and Oprah. And I felt that my father was surely amused.

After davening, my driver took me to the *Oprah* show. I was met by Lisa, a black woman in her thirties. She got straight to the point.

"You had a minyan?"

"Yes, thank you," I said.

"Was it properly Orthodox? Did you say Kaddish?"

"Absolutely. Couldn't be better," I answered.

She looked at me with that look that star surgeons have when they come out of the operating room. Or maybe it's the look that battle commanders have when coming back from a military operation. It's a look that says, "Nothing is too complicated."

I was on *Oprah*. She was very professional. I had my five minutes of fame. But all I can remember of that day is the Kaddish.

Will Somebody Say Kaddish with Me?

Avron Shore

My mother no longer comprehends what is going on around her. She is almost one hundred years old. Until recently, she was a vibrant, bustling individual who not only enjoyed life but gladdened the hearts of the many who knew her. I can say without question that she has been a wonderful mother — in my eyes the best — but now she is as helpless as a baby.

I doubt if she knows that I feed her lunch every day, but I do know at some deep level she understands that I will perform the ultimate mitzvah for her. After she has gone on to the next world, I will say Kaddish for her. But I have to qualify that wish — because it would be more accurate to say I hope I will be able to say Kaddish for her, because it might not be possible. It is getting harder and harder to find a minyan. Unless a bar or bat mitzvah is celebrated, our synagogues are never full on Shabbat. What is heartbreaking is struggling to find a minyan for *minchah* or *ma'ariv* in the winter. Too many Jewish men no longer make it a practice to go to shul on a regular basis or make it part of their schedules to drop in to be part of a minyan.

In order for Kaddish to be said, you require a minyan, ten adult males. It is recited on behalf of all of the Jewish people, emphasizing our common responsibility and our interlinked fates. By saying Kaddish, you are first honoring G-d, and then you are honoring your father and your mother.

Over the years, I have often been part of a minyan. I have seen this sacred duty performed for a friend, a relative, and even a stranger. I have never seen it as an imposition or a hardship. Rather, it has helped to strengthen me and to assist in my understanding of who I really am: a Jew. Our synagogues have wonderful members who have fulfilled their responsibilities and have said Kaddish for their parents. But sadly, they now see their own children not fulfilling this obligation and having their children, the grandchildren, witness this lapse.

What this problem says to me is that somewhere along the way, we may have lost our sense of responsibility for one another. I know we have busy lives. Work demands a lot from us. Most of us consider our families more important than strangers. But in perspective, the Jewish people form such a minuscule percentage of the 6 billion people on this planet. In one way or another, we are all interconnected and are not really strangers.

Yes, life we like to say is "demanding" and "hard," but in the last sixty years, life on the whole has been good for those of us fortunate to live in the Western World. We haven't had to worry about pogroms or closed doors, except for the odd private club. So many times, we don't feel a need or urgency to do all the little things that define us as Jews. For those of us who are not Orthodox, we don't look identifiably Jewish. We no longer carry out the 613 commandments, let alone the big ten.

But you have to stop and ask yourself: how many commandments can we violate or not carry out before we are no longer Jews? It seems to me that particularly those commandments associated with the "life cycle" — birth to death — remind us of who we are. We hold a bris for our baby boys. We help our sons prepare for their bar mitzvahs. We get married under a *chuppah*. And when our parents die, we say Kaddish.

It is a sad day when a parent dies. But if a mourner cannot say Kaddish, imagine how this only adds unnecessarily to his distress. To be part of a minyan only takes about thirty minutes out of your day. If you make a commitment to come to shul only one day a month — one day — it would make a BIG difference to the shul. First, you would be doing a mitzvah by giving comfort to those who have to say Kaddish. Second, you would be teaching your children, by example, the importance of fulfilling the mitzvah. And third, it is like life insurance — you will be increasing the likelihood of someone saying Kaddish for you.

Surely this is a mitzvah you can live with: thirty minutes one day a month, twelve times a year. Or maybe our synagogues will make it part of your commitment: once becoming a member, you must perform "Jewry duty" one week every year.

So help a fellow Jew perform his obligation. He can't do it alone.

Concepts
of Kaddish

A Practical Guide to Kaddish

Rabbi Gedalia Zweig

Kaddish is one last honor one can give to the deceased. When we say Kaddish for our parents, we are fulfilling the mitzvah of *kibbud ad va'em*, honoring one's father and mother. Some say that honoring parents after they pass away is a bigger mitzvah than honoring them during their lifetime. During their lifetime, one might honor them only out of fear or in order to make sure they will not lose their inheritance. But after they die, it's solely *l'shem Shamayim* (for the sake of Heaven).

The exact origins of Kaddish are unknown, but the opening words of this prayer are inspired by the verse in *Yechezkel* 38:23. The central passage, "*Yehei Shemei rabba mevorach l'olam u'le'olmei olmaya* — May His great Name be blessed forever and ever," is an approximate Aramaic translation of the famous declaration of Yaakov Avinu, *"Baruch Shem kevod malchuto l'olam va'ed* — Blessed is His holy Name forever and ever" (Talmud, *Berachot*). Yaakov's children wanted to show their father that they were not affected by the idol worship of Egypt. As their father lay on his deathbed, they proclaimed, *"Shema Yisrael Hashem Elokeinu Hashem Echad* — Hear, Israel [Yaakov's name given by the Almighty] the Lord is our G-d, the Lord is One!" Yaakov responded: "Blessed is His holy Name forever and ever!"

The Midrash says that by reciting Kaddish, one elevates the soul of the departed and redeems it from Gehinnom. It brings eternal life to the soul for whom the Kaddish is said. It also brings great merit to the ones saying it — the Talmud states that one who says, *"Yehei Shemei rabba..."* in a loud voice merits to be free of sins for seventy years (Talmud, *Berachot*).

The mourner first says the Mourner's Kaddish at the funeral and then continues to say Kaddish for eleven months. The Hebrew word *hesped*, the eulogy said at a funeral, is similar to the word *hefsed*, loss. A eulogy is an expression of the great loss that is felt from the death of the loved one. The loss is not only of a loved one, but also the loss of Jewish tradition and commitment buried with that loved one. By saying Kaddish, the mourner reaffirms his belief in G-d and his resolve to continue the Jewish tradition.

But the Kaddish prayer makes no mention of death or grief. The Sages ask, "Why then does a mourner say it every day?" After the death of a loved one, a person may feel bitter and reject G-d. The Kaddish is a prayer of praise to the Almighty. By proclaiming, *"Yehei Shemei rabba... —* May His great Name be blessed forever and ever," the mourner acknowledges that the death of the loved one is G-d's will and he accepts G-d's judgment as righteous. (This is also the reason we say, *"Baruch Dayan ha'emet —* Blessed is the Almighty, the true Judge," when we hear of someone's death.)

The purpose of Kaddish is to sanctify and exalt G-d's Name. For this reason it must be said in a public forum — in a minyan of ten — and the central passage of the Kaddish, *"Yehei Shemei rabba mevorach l'olam u'le'olmei olmaya —* May His great Name be blessed forever and ever," is said out loud by the entire congregation. This passage has the same amount of words (seven) and the same number of letters (twenty-eight) as two other very important verses in the Torah. The first verse in the Torah, *"Bereishit bara Elokim et hashamayim v'et ha'aretz —* In the beginning G-d created the heavens and the earth," has seven words and twenty-eight Hebrew letters, as does the verse that introduces *mattan Torah*: *"Vayedaber Elokim et kol hadevarim leimor —* And G-d spoke all these words, saying." Every time we say *"Yehei Shemei rabba..."* in Kaddish, we become partners in the Creation and it is as if we are receiving the Torah anew.

Laws and Customs

- Mourners recite *Kaddish Yatom* (Mourner's Kaddish) at the funeral and children say it for eleven months from the day of a parent's death. For a child, a spouse, or an in-law, one says Kaddish for thirty days.

- Kaddish is said at least seven times — ideally four times during the morning service and three times during *minchah* and *ma'ariv* (including the Rabbis' Kaddish between *minchah* and *ma'ariv*).

- One may recite Kaddish anywhere there is a minyan of ten or more Jewish males age thirteen and above. This can be at a business meeting, school, or family gathering — anywhere ten men can gather.

- If a mourner arrives in the middle of a service and Kaddish is being said, he should start Kaddish from the beginning and end at his own pace.

- If a mourner can't find a minyan and the time to say Kaddish has passed, while it is not a substitute for Kaddish, he can say *Tehillim*, chapter 119. He should recite the verses that correspond to the letters in the person's name. For example, for someone named David, he should recite the verses that begin with *dalet*, then *vav*, then *dalet* again. Another option, if one cannot find a minyan, is to study a *mishnah* in the person's memory. *Mikva'ot* is very common for this purpose, as is *Pirkei Avot* (found after Shabbat afternoon service).

- At the end of any service, after *Aleinu*, the Mourner's Kaddish should be recited even if no mourners are present. It should be recited by either the chazzan or by someone whose parents are not alive or have not expressed their objection to him reciting Kaddish.

- Many shuls have a custom to let everyone who must say Kaddish lead their own minyan. One who serves as chazzan gets the merit of the entire minyan when the others answer, "*Yehei Shemei rabba*... — May His great Name be blessed..."

- Many people sponsor a special *kiddush* on the last day they say Kaddish.

I have seen many people say Kaddish in tears. This is a healthy sign. A person who begins weeping while saying Kaddish should be encouraged to finish each word, and others should wait for him. Thoughts come to mind about time spent together, words that were said and maybe things that should- n't have been said. Remember that you are doing the greatest kindness for your loved one by reciting the praises of G-d con- tained in the Kaddish.

After Kaddish

Eleven months of mourning have ended. For almost a year you've been waking up early to go to a morning minyan and adjusting your dinner schedule to say Kaddish. Now it's over. What do you do?

Many people would agree that after almost a year of at- tending shul, you'd find it easy to continue. There is nothing wrong with continuing to attend services regularly. No doubt you've made new friends, or perhaps others are now relying on you to help make a minyan so they can say Kaddish. You've been a steady customer. Don't stop going.

Kaddish FAQ's

Rabbi Chanan Yitzchaki

Q: Can Kaddish be said in English (or any other language)?

A: By the letter of the law, yes. But we say it in Aramaic so that the angels won't understand it, and so that there will be one universal language for the Kaddish.

Q: Can you say Kaddish for a brother or sister — that is, for someone other than a parent?

A: Yes, if no one else says it. For any loved one other than a parent (son, daughter, wife, brother, or sister), Kaddish is said for thirty days.

Rabbi Chanan Yitzchaki is a former teacher at the Community Hebrew Academy of Toronto. He now lives in Israel.

Q: If you miss the prayer service, and hence saying Kaddish, can you still say Kaddish?

A: Yes, if there is a minyan of ten males age 13 and over.

Q: Some people say Kaddish more slowly than others. How slow can you say it?

A: Take all the time you need. Say it as fast or as slowly as you like. Finish after the congregation if necessary.

Q: If you miss a service entirely, what can you do?

A: Find out where a service is taking place and give them a call, asking that Kaddish be said for the person. For example, if it's 10 a.m. in Toronto and you've missed *shacharit*, you can call Los Angeles, where it's 7 a.m., and ask someone at a minyan to say Kaddish for Dina bat Yosef (that is, use the person's father's name). If this is impossible, learn a *mishnah* or other section of the Torah in memory of the person.

Q: What if, G-d forbid, a second parent dies within the eleven-month Kaddish period for the person's other parent (for example, if a person's mother dies within eleven months of the death of his father)?

A: The custom is that we don't say Kaddish on the first or last days of the twelfth month. There is a *gemara* (*Shabbat* 33) that says, "The judgment for the wicked is twelve months." We never suspect our parents are included among the wicked — therefore we say

Kaddish for eleven months. The exception is that if the second death falls within the *shivah* period, then we say Kaddish until eleven months after the death of the second parent.

Q. If a parent loses a young child, should he say Kaddish?

A. If the child was less than thirty days old, a parent is not obligated to say Kaddish.

Q. If two people both have a *yahrtzeit* and want to lead the service, what should be done?

A. Rav Shlomo Aviner of Ateret Kohanim and Beit El says that *nachat ruach*, "making peace for the soul of the departed," takes precedence over any honor a person may desire. So they should try to resolve the impasse amicably. Ideally, if each one can find nine others, they should each form and lead their own minyan.

קדיש יתום

יִתְגַּדַּל וְיִתְקַדַּשׁ שְׁמֵהּ רַבָּא. (אָמֵן.) בְּעָלְמָא דִּי בְרָא כִרְעוּתֵהּ.
וְיַמְלִיךְ מַלְכוּתֵהּ, וְיַצְמַח פֻּרְקָנֵהּ וִיקָרֵב מְשִׁיחֵהּ. (אָמֵן.) בְּחַיֵּיכוֹן
וּבְיוֹמֵיכוֹן וּבְחַיֵּי דְכָל בֵּית יִשְׂרָאֵל, בַּעֲגָלָא וּבִזְמַן קָרִיב. וְאִמְרוּ:
אָמֵן.

אָמֵן. יְהֵא שְׁמֵהּ רַבָּא מְבָרַךְ לְעָלַם וּלְעָלְמֵי עָלְמַיָּא.
יְהֵא שְׁמֵהּ רַבָּא מְבָרַךְ לְעָלַם וּלְעָלְמֵי עָלְמַיָּא.

יִתְבָּרַךְ וְיִשְׁתַּבַּח וְיִתְפָּאַר וְיִתְרוֹמַם וְיִתְנַשֵּׂא וְיִתְהַדָּר וְיִתְעַלֶּה
וְיִתְהַלָּל שְׁמֵהּ דְּקוּדְשָׁא בְּרִיךְ הוּא (בְּרִיךְ הוּא) לְעֵלָּא מִן כָּל
בִּרְכָתָא וְשִׁירָתָא תֻּשְׁבְּחָתָא וְנֶחֱמָתָא, דַּאֲמִירָן בְּעָלְמָא. וְאִמְרוּ:
אָמֵן. (אָמֵן.)

יְהֵא שְׁלָמָא רַבָּא מִן שְׁמַיָּא, וְחַיִּים עָלֵינוּ וְעַל כָּל יִשְׂרָאֵל. וְאִמְרוּ:
אָמֵן. (אָמֵן.)

עֹשֶׂה שָׁלוֹם בִּמְרוֹמָיו, הוּא יַעֲשֶׂה שָׁלוֹם עָלֵינוּ, וְעַל כָּל יִשְׂרָאֵל.
וְאִמְרוּ: אָמֵן. (אָמֵן.)

The Mourner's Kaddish

May His great Name grow greater and become sanctified in the world He created as He willed. May the Kingship rule in your lifetimes and your days and in the lifetimes of the entire house of Israel, speedily and very soon, and let us say Amen.

May His great Name be blessed forever and ever.

May the Holy One's Name be blessed, praised, exalted, extolled, honored, upraised, and lauded, blessed is He, beyond any blessing and song, praise and consolation that are uttered in the world, and let us say Amen.

May the One who brings peace in high places bring peace upon us and all of Israel. And let us say Amen.

Here are two of the most popular versions of the Kaddish.
(Consult your rabbi to advise which one you should use.)

Ashkenazic Pronunciation:

Yisgadal v'yiskadash Shemei rabba.

Congregation answers: Amen.

B'olma di vra chirusei v'yamlich malchusei b'chayeichon u'veyomeichon u'vechayei d'chol beis Yisrael ba'agala u'vizeman kariv v'imru Amen.

Congregation answers: Amen Yehei Shemei rabba mevorach l'olam u'le'olmei olmaya.

Yehei shemei rabba mevorach l'olam u'le'olmei olmaya.

Yisbarach v'yishtabach v'yispa'ar v'yisromam v'yisnasei v'yis-hadar v'yis-aleh v'yis-hallal Shemei dikudesha *(pause)* berich Hu.

Congregation answers: Berich Hu.

L'eila min kol birchasa v'shirasa tushbechasa v'nechemasa da'amiran b'olma v'imru Amen.

Congregation answers: Amen.

Yehei shelama rabba min shemaya v'chaim aleinu v'al kol Yisrael v'imru Amen.

Congregation answers: Amen.

Take three steps backward. Bow left when saying "oseh," bow right when saying "shalom," and bow forward from "v'al kol" until "amen."

Oseh shalom bimromav Hu ya'aseh shalom aleinu v'al kol Yisrael v'imru Amen.

Congregation answers: Amen.

Remain standing in place for a few moments, then take three steps forward.

Sefardic Pronunciation:

Yitgadal v'yitkadash Shemei rabba.

Congregation answers: Amen.

B'olma di vra chirutei v'yamlich malchutei v'yatzmach purkanei v'kareiv meshichei b'chayeichon u'veyomeichon u'vechayei d'chol beit Yisrael ba'agala u'vizeman kariv v'imru Amen.

Congregation answers: Amen yehei Shemei rabba mevorach l'olam u'le'olmei olmaya.

Yehei Shemei rabba mevorach l'olam u'le'olmei olmaya.

Yitbarach v'yishtabach v'yitpa'ar v'yitromam v'yitnasei v'yit-hadar v'yit-aleh v'yit-hallal Shemei dikudesha (*pause*) berich Hu.

Congregation answers: Berich Hu.

L'eila min kol birchata v'shirata tushbechata v'nechemata da'amiran b'olma v'imru Amen.

Congregation answers: Amen.

Yehei shelama rabba min shemaya v'chaim aleinu v'al kol Yisrael v'imru Amen.

Congregation answers: Amen.

Take three steps backward. Bow left when saying "oseh," bow right when saying "shalom," and bow forward from "v'al kol" until "amen."

Oseh shalom bimromav Hu ya'aseh shalom aleinu v'al kol Yisrael v'imru Amen.

Congregation answers: Amen.

Remain standing in place for a few moments, then take three steps forward.

Glossary

Aleinu — Prayer said at the end of every prayer service. Kaddish is recited right after it.

aliyat neshamot — Literally, "the raising up of souls to Heaven"; saying Kaddish to elevate the soul of the departed.

am ha'aretz — One who is unknowledgeable of Jewish laws.

Amidah — The *Shemoneh Esrei* or "standing" prayer. It consists of nineteen blessings and is said three times daily.

ba'al teshuvah — A person who becomes more observant of mitzvot.

ba'al tefillah — The person who leads the prayer service.

"Barchu et Hashem" — The first words of the blessing for the Torah reading.

b'ezrat Hashem — with G-d's help.

Berachot — One of the sections of the Talmud studied during the thirty-day mourning period; also the plural of "blessings" in Hebrew.

bikur cholim — The mitzvah of visiting the sick.

"b'rov am" — A majority of the people.

Chabad — Initials for *chochmah* (wisdom), *binah* (understanding), and *da'at* (knowledge), used to refer to Lubavitch Jews and the Lubavitch chassidic movement.

Chazon Ish — Rabbi Avraham Yeshayah Karelitz (1878–1953), one of the most revered sages of the twentieth century.

chiyuv — Obligation; duty.

chol hamo'ed — The interim days of the holidays of Sukkot (Feast of the Tabernacles) and Pesach (Passover), the days between the first and last two days of both holidays.

davening — Yiddish word for "praying."

Hashem — Literally, "the Name," meaning G-d.

Kaddish — Prayer that is said for eleven months after a parent dies or thirty days after another close relative dies.

Kaddish D'Rabbanan — Rabbis' Kaddish. Unlike the Mourner's Kaddish, this Kaddish may be said anytime after a word of learning (such as a *mishnah* or a halachah).

kapote — Yiddish word for "black coat."

Kedushah — Part of the Amidah, the standing prayer.

kiddush Hashem — Sanctifying G-d's Name by being a good example.

kippah — Skullcap or head covering worn by Jewish males.

kollel — Full-time yeshivah study for married men.

Lechah Dodi — Song chanted on Friday night to welcome the Sabbath.

ma'ariv — Evening prayer service.

mechitzah — The physical divider that separates men and women during prayer services.

Mikva'ot — One of the sections of the Talmud studied during the thirty-day mourning period.

minchah — Afternoon prayer service.

minhag — Custom.

minyan — A group of ten Jewish men above the age of thirteen.

Mishnah — The Oral Law, divided into six volumes, compiled by the Sage Rabbi Yehudah HaNasi.

neshamah — Soul.

rebbetzin — Wife of a rabbi.

seudah — Meal.

Shabbat — Saturday; the Sabbath; the seventh day of the week, a day of rest.

Shabbaton — A large get-together on the Sabbath.

shacharit — Morning prayer service.

shomer mitzvot — One who observes the Jewish laws.

siddur — Prayer book.

siyum mishnayot — The completion of a tractate of the Oral Law after the thirty-day mourning period.

tallit — Prayer shawl.

tefillah — Prayer.

tefillin — Prayer straps worn for prayer except on the Sabbath and holidays.

yahrtzeit — Yiddish word for the yearly anniversary of the death of a loved one.

yarmulke — Yiddish for skullcap or head covering worn by Jewish males.

yatom — Orphan.

yishuv — Small town.

zichron — Memory.